**Begin your journey today with
a FREE copy of MOONLIGHT FALLS,
the first novel in the Thriller and Shamus
Award winning series. Or visit
www.VincentZandri.com to join Vincent's
"For your eyes only" newsletter today.**

PRAISE FOR VINCENT ZANDRI

"Sensational . . . masterful . . . brilliant."
—New York Post

"(A) chilling tale of obsessive love from Thriller
Award–winner Zandri (Moonlight Weeps) . . .
Riveting."
—Publishers Weekly

". . . Oh, what a story it is . . . Riveting . . . A terrific
old school thriller."
—Booklist "Starred Review"

"My fear level rose with this Zandri novel like it
hasn't done before. Wondering what the killer had
in store for Jude and seeing the ending, well, this is
one book that will be with me for a long time to
come!"
—Reviews by Molly

"I very highly recommend this book . . . It's a great
crime drama that is full of action and intense
suspense, along with some great twists . . . Vincent

Zandri has become a huge name and just keeps pouring out one best seller after another."
—Life in Review

"(*The Innocent*) is a thriller that has depth and substance, wickedness and compassion."
—The Times-Union (Albany)

"The action never wanes."
—Fort Lauderdale Sun-Sentinel

"Gritty, fast-paced, lyrical and haunting."
—Harlan Coben, New York Times bestselling author of *Six Years*

"Tough, stylish, heartbreaking."
—Don Winslow, New York Times bestselling author of *Savages* and *Cartel.*

"A tightly crafted, smart, disturbing, elegantly crafted complex thriller . . . I dare you to start it and not keep reading."
—MJ Rose, New York Times bestselling author of *Halo Effect* and *Closure*

"A classic slice of raw pulp noir . . ."
—William Landay, New York Times bestselling author of *Defending Jacob*

Pieces of Mind: Fictional Truths and Non-Fictional Lies about Writing and the Writing Life

VINCENT ZANDRI

Pieces of Mind

"Writing is its own reward."

Henry Miller

Pieces of Mind

Introduction

Back when I was a kid, the last thing I ever thought I would be when I grew up was a writer—and a fairly successful one at that. That is, a writer who is successful enough not to have to drag his ass out of bed every Monday morning on account of a day job. That's right; I don't have to work for *the man* because *I am* the man. But then, despite the obvious perks like freedom, for instance, there is a downside to working entirely for yourself . . . Nah, on second thought, there really isn't a downside at all.

So, back to when I was a kid.

I grew up in a household where my dad—a commercial construction business owner—made the money, and my mother stayed at home to raise the kids. He came home around four thirty, and we promptly ate dinner at five. By six, the kitchen had been cleaned and the day's clothing was being traded in for pajamas. In bed at eight, where I devoured all sorts of comic books, novels, and even World War II history volumes. Lights were out by nine. My dad would be up at dark thirty, which is when I would wake up, and we'd do it all over again.

To say that my dad's business and work ethic consumed all the oxygen in the household would be putting it lightly. Our lives revolved around it. Nothing was ever scheduled without the business in mind. The fact that it came first, before everything else, there was no doubt. Family meals, religious obligations, holidays, and family vacations all revolved around my dad's construction business, and the time he needed to put into it.

So, naturally, when I was born, the first thing my father said to my mother while she lay exhausted and bleeding on the hospital bed, was this: "We can stop having children now. We have a boy, and he will carry on the business."

It was a strange way for me to grow up, always knowing in the back and fore of my head that I would one day be running a construction company just like my dad. And I guess, looking back on it all these years later, I probably enjoyed the novelty of it all. The sense that I had one up on my friends who would have no choice but to look for jobs when they grew up. It probably provided me with a kind of arrogance and edge—something that accompanied me all through college.

But by then, some significant cracks had appeared in what, up until then, had been a solid-as-a-rock plan. By the time I turned twenty-one, I had spent five summers working in the field for Zandri Construction Corp. I even injured myself on several occasions, the major incident occurring when I stepped on a six-penny nail, the business end of which was sticking straight up out of demolished floorboard. It impaled itself through my foot entirely.

Did it hurt? You bet.

But the physical pain was nothing compared to the ribbing I endured from the other workers, most of whom at that time were Viet Nam vets who had seen some pretty bad things over "in the shit." Curiously, and sadly, most if not all of those poor souls went to early graves due to alcoholism and despair. But my dad, himself a vet, maintained a soft spot in his heart for them, so he always made sure to employ vets whenever he could.

I digress.

Having a taste of the business from the point of view of a laborer didn't do a whole lot for my love of the construction business. In fact, if anything, it made me dread it. My old man put me on the worst of the worst jobs. Cleaning concrete forms in the hot summer sun for eight hours at a time. Hefting wheel barrel loads of wet concrete from point A to point B until my back and shoulders were on fire (a good way to get in shape for high school football season it turns out). Shoveling ditches. Tearing out and disposing of asbestos with no masks (I have the scars on my lungs to prove it, or so a recent MRI proved).

One particular job that remains fresh in my memory is cleaning out the waste receiving pit located directly below a commercial paper making machine. A pit filled with so much watery filth and toxic discharge that we had to wear fishermen's waders while we formed a kind of pale brigade, emptying the pit one pale load at a time. It was the only time I never made it through the day since I couldn't prevent myself from gagging and eventually puking my guts out.

So, yes, I grew to hate the business . . . with a passion, in fact. You might ask: why would your dad put you in a position to hate a business he so badly wanted you to take over? The answer is this: there was a method to his madness.

Years later, when I'd already become a journalist and author, we took a long walk on a beach in Cape Cod. He explained to me that by making me work the same kind of crap jobs that he'd had to endure as a young man, he was instilling not only character but something much more practical. If I developed a hatred for the worst kind of physical labor possible, I would finish my education. Something he was unable to do since he had a young wife and even a child to support at only twenty-one years old.

He also told me that I would be much more interested in making the transition from the field to the office part of the business. Something that occurred immediately upon my graduation from Providence College in 1986.

If my first day working in the office of the construction company was any indicator, I wasn't going to like that part of the business any better than I did the field. The shocking thing was, I hated it even more. At least working in the field provided physical stimulation. However, in the office going over bills and blueprints, finger tapping an adding machine, making calls about lengths of lumber and quantities of brick and concrete block, I wanted to hang myself from the rafters. From the outset, I knew the work was not for me.

It was at that time I started my real education. I was devouring novels and books by writers I'd never had the chance to read while working on my "formal education." I read Tolstoy, Max Frisch, Jim Harrison, Raymond Carver, Tim O'Brien, Martha Gelhorn, Scott Fitzgerald, Thomas Wolf (and Tom Wolf), Norman Mailer, and of course, Ernest Hemingway.

I loved Hemingway's work, especially the short stories from *In Our Time*. I felt that his prose spoke to me and me alone. It was the first time I had ever been exposed to real magic happening on the page. Yes, I had read Hemingway in high school, but this was different. I was reading him for the first time again, with a new set of eyes—eyes that belonged to a young man with his entire future ahead of him.

The future.

There it was again. The F word. And there I was working in a field that not only rejected creativity, but was dependent on the accuracy and efficiency of engineering equations. It was a business of numbers and calculations, and I was terrible at math. I was then barely twenty-two years old and rapidly falling in love not only with words and books but authors and their lives. I wanted to know what it took for someone like Hemingway to become a famous writer. How did he do it? Did he just wake up one day and start hammering out a story on his Remington portable typewriter? Did he go to writing school? Did he ever want to do anything else with his life?

I began to devour as many biographies of the great writers as I could. Hemingway once again led the effort. I read everything I could about his life, from his birth in 1899 to his tragic suicide in 1961. The stuff I encountered was so wonderful, so adventurous, so romantic, so 180-degrees apart from the life I was leading that I could barely wait to get off work so I could continue reading about the life I would eventually attempt to emulate, in my own particular way.

I read about Papa Hemingway fly fishing in the Fox River, handing out chocolates to soldiers in the Italian trenches during WWI, suffering a terrible injury after a mortar shell exploded beside him, and recovering in a hospital not far

Vincent Zandri

from Milan where he fell in love with a nurse years older than him.

Then I read about his early days in Paris as a struggling writer and foreign correspondent. There were the bullfights in Spain, big game fishing in Key West and Cuba, big game hunting in East Africa, the Spanish Civil War, D-Day and World War II, back to Paris and Venice and China, and wine, women, and song. It was a life lived so prodigiously and so fully that it took my breath away, and still does to this day.

Would Hemingway waste his time in a four-walled office punching an adding machine?

You know the answer to that one.

By the end of that first summer working for Zandri Construction Corp., I had made a decision. I was going to do whatever it took to become a writer. I was going to give up the business opportunity of a lifetime and invest my life in pursuit not only of letters but also living life as well as I could live it. I would waste no opportunity to experience everything I could in order to write about it later.

I would taste it, feel it, smell it, hear it, laugh with it, cry with it, sleep with it, live with it. I would break free of the bonds of my life and travel the world, sail the seas, fly the skies, ride the wave of freedom that only the writing life could offer.

I would break free of convention and familial expectations.

In the end, I said goodbye to my dad's business, but it was only the start of something incredibly new and exciting. I not only loved writing, but I was also a fan of writers and writing. Hell, I even started

collecting old manual typewriters—
something I still do to this day.

I'd go on to write for the local
newspaper, the local magazines, then
graduate to the literary journals, and
small presses. I'd enroll in prestigious
writing programs like Bread Loaf Writer's
Colony and the New York State Writer's
Institute. Later on, I'd earn an MFA in
Writing from Vermont College. Soon after
that, I wrote my first big novel, nailed the
hotshot New York agent who scored the
mega first novel deal with Delacorte Press
for my novel, *The Innocent (As Catch Can)*.
That two book hard and soft contract was
worth a quarter of a million bucks. I'd
made it.

I was not yet thirty-three years old.

What followed were some serious
rollercoaster-like up and down years, but
also years that were more

Hemingwayesque than I might have originally bargained for. There were the marriages and divorces, the kids, the houses, and cars. There were the travels, which took me to exotic locales like Africa, Egypt, Morocco, Peru, China, India, Nepal, and months at a time in Florence, Italy, the city that has become my second home.

I've written in Paris, Rome, Innsbruck, Istanbul, Athens, London, Bilbao, Jerusalem, Cotonou West Africa, Moscow, Hong Kong, Guatemala City, Lima, and that's what comes immediately to mind. I've nearly drowned in the Ganges, was almost crushed to death when our truck was purposely run off the road in post-revolutionary Egypt, have been bitten by piranhas in the Amazon Jungle, stared down angry soldiers in the West African bush country, and traveled by elephant in Nepal's Chitwan National Forest.

As of this writing, I spend upwards of four months per year away from home. Travel is a passion that has not abated with age, but in fact, grown stronger. Not bad for a man who, thirty years ago, faced a lifetime of four walls for ten hours per day and two weeks of vacation per year whether I liked it or not.

In this volume, you'll find essays not only on writing, but also the writing life which can take many forms be it an observation of the world as I see it at that particular time or a travel piece on Italy. I wrestled with making this a sort of chronological omnibus of my non-fiction writing, starting with some of my most sophomoric pieces. These include, but are not limited to, reports on high school football games, fly fishing essays, bird hunting features, book reviews and the like for publications such as *The Times*

Union Newspaper (Albany), New York Newsday, Hudson Valley Magazine, Game and Fish Magazine, RT, and others. I also considered including some early literary fiction published in private and academic journals like *Negative Capability, Fugue, Old Hickory Review, The Maryland Review, Rosebud, Buffalo Spree,* and *Orange Coast Magazine.*

But in the end, I decided to go with pieces that appeared in *The Vincent Zandri Vox* for two simple reasons. Firstly, these essays are more recent and, therefore, more accomplished; and second, they are a reflection of the new era of publishing which arguably began in late 2007 with the introduction of the Kindle eReader and soon after, the Amazon KDP independent author platform.

The pieces are edgy, at times funny, other times sad, often angry, entirely anti-politically correct, but above all informative. Read them for what they might teach you, or read them for fun. Hopefully, you will do a little of both.

    Today, I have twenty-six novels and novellas in print both traditionally and independently, plus numerous short stories, boxed sets, translations, and anthologies. This is my first non-fiction collection, and I'm choosing to publish it under my own indie label, Bear Media, simply because it will be delivered to market much faster. I've hit the *New York Times*, *USA Today*, and Amazon No. 1 Overall Bestseller lists, sold close to a million copies of my novels and stories, won the ITW Thriller and PWA Shamus Awards for Best Paperback Novel, and been featured in *The New York Times*, on Fox News, Bloomberg TV, and nearly made it to CBS's Sixty Minutes, but that fell through. I'm considered an outlier by some—or an outlaw—in that I don't stick to any one publisher or publishing method, but instead do things my way, on my terms. A theme you will see repeated again and again throughout this volume that predominantly includes essays from 2009 all the way through 2011. This was a golden period for indie authors in that it was still possible to make a ton of money on a good novel simply by lowering the price to $0.99. Those days are gone now, but I still see the enormous potential of indie publishing for writers like me who are work-horse prolific.

You'll read the essays as I wrote them, warts and all. I felt that rewriting them would be disingenuous in some mildly profound way, like colorizing Casablanca just because technology has made it possible. But in all disclosure, I have, in specific instances, deleted names of certain publishers and other publishing associates for both legal and personal purposes. But this small edit in no way affects the spirit and tone of the piece.

I've come a long way since I first entered into business with my dad. There are days I still can't believe how things turned out. It took a gargantuan effort to break the bonds of family and what had been expected of me as my dad's only son. For a while, it was hard, and our relationship suffered because of my decisions to leave the family fold for what became my true calling. But in the end, I know he was proud of me and my accomplishments. He also saw in me something he wished he had seen in himself—the ability to throw caution to the wind and go for it.

Not long before his death, he pulled me aside and said, "You know, I envy you.

You're like your grandfather. You don't let anything bother you for too long. You let it slide off your back while you keep on going. Me, I'm not like that. I *can't* be like that. I sweat the small stuff. Always have, always will."

Six months later my dad died of a massive coronary while tying his work boots. He was 76 years old and still working a sixty-hour week trying to keep his construction business afloat and his family happy.

Whether that's one of my fictional truths or truthful fictions doesn't matter, because the point is this: Life is short, spend it wisely. Chase after your passion, whatever it is. For death, in all its bleak finality, is indeed on your heels every minute of every day.

Vincent Zandri

May 30, 2017

Antigua, Guatemala

Biting the Nail: The Discipline of Writing

"Where do you get your discipline?"

That's the question I'm asked most frequently about my solitary writing life. Most people who work according the programmed schedule of job and career find it inconceivable that a person can actually roll out of bed, face a blank page, and begin to make words. Yet, as writers, that's what we do. We create and in order to create we have to have discipline. Discipline to work alone, according to our own rules, according to our own high standards, according to our own priorities and curiosities.

Acquiring discipline isn't so hard when you are passionate about your work—when you have a desire not only to write well, but to do it better than anyone has done it before. At the same time you have to develop a skin of armor in order to feed the obsession. The first most important lesson of the disciplined writing life is learning that you're not always going to be successful. Most of the time you will fail and must face the resulting rejection head on. That's the most difficult thing about discipline: carrying on with your work unabated, even in the face of rejection.

So where does my discipline come from?

As clichéd as it sounds, I can only tell you that it comes from deep inside. It's not something I have to work up, so much as it's something I have to feed on a daily basis. Discipline means waking up early every day, day in and day out, and writing. It's writing every day in isolation no matter what's happening in my life. Be it sick kids, angry spouses, insolvent bank accounts, a broken toilet, a terrorist attack . . . I write no matter what. Hemingway called this sometimes impossible but necessary process, "biting the nail." And anyone who has the discipline to write every day no matter what, understands what biting the nail is all about. Writing, like the discipline it requires, can be an awfully painful process.

Back in 1992, I wrote in my published essay, *A Literary Life*, "In the morning, weariness begins with darkness. It surrounds me inside my kitchen like a weighted shroud, cumbersome and black. It continues as my fingertips search and locate a light switch next to the telephone, above my son's hi-chair. White light stings my eyes when I flip it up. There is a clock above the sink . . . I interpret a big hand

and little hand that have not yet made 6:00AM."

Those were the days when I wrote in the mornings, worked a fulltime job and received rejections every day. But still, I crawled out of bed and wrote. I guess all these years later, I can truthfully say, discipline is what I had in the place of sleep, in the place of comfort, in the place of security and success. Discipline was and remains the bedfellow I seek when I am at my most lonely.

Eventually the discipline would reap its rewards.

In the 12 years since I've earned my MFA from Vermont College, I've published three novels, with one on the way this winter. I've been translated into numerous languages. I've published almost two dozen short stories, countless articles, essays and blogs. I've traveled "on assignment" to China, Turkey, Greece,

Italy, France, Spain, Africa and more. Along the way I've met wonderful people, seen wonderful things, witnessed atrocities, unspeakable disease, hunger and corruption. I've written about much of it. Some of it, I've simply stored away in my brain for some future story or novel down the road.

For all its rewards, discipline demands stiff payment.

Because of my priorities, I've failed at two marriages and many more relationships. I've lost friends and lost the faith and trust of family members who have come to think of me as unreliable or flaky at best. Because after all, I tend to use a holiday like Christmas as a time to work, and when family events like birthdays come up, I might be traveling or locked up in my studio with my significant other . . . Well, you know her name. It starts with a D.

I have managed however, to find a way to balance time with my kids. Not that it's always been easy. Children are a distraction, no bones about it. But they are also fuel for your discipline. I'm not entirely certain that I could have achieved any kind of success without them. Children open up emotional vaults that would otherwise remain sealed shut. You need to expose the contents of these vaults in your prose.

My writing simply wouldn't be the same without kids. Now that they're almost grown up, I still keep them as close as possible without smothering them. When it comes to my children, my philosophy has always been, hug them, tell them you love them, and make them laugh once a day. You'd be surprised how well this works. Also, don't be afraid to tell them the truth. They know when you're lying. If you can't spend time with them because you have to feed the discipline, be honest about it. They will appreciate you for it and come to respect you.

Case and point: it's a beautiful Saturday afternoon and I'm writing this article. My children are home, just outside the closed door of my studio, where I can hear them engaged in some sort of friendly argument. I'm not doing anything with them per se. But I'm here with them, for them.

This month alone I will write and publish 36 short architecture and construction articles, three major blogs, present a revised version of *The Concrete Pearl* (my fifth novel) to my agent, write one or two features, engage in pre-publicity for *Moonlight Falls*, and maybe, if there's time, pen a new piece for my personal blog. In between all this, I'll juggle time with the kids, time for exercise, time to tip some beers with friends, time for a few road trips, time to be by myself and read. Have I mentioned the discipline required to read books?

One word of warning, the discipline, no matter how beautiful a bedfellow, does not always respond lovingly. Even after you've scored a major book contract or two. During my second marriage, I suffered through a writer's block that lasted five long years, a period during which I published not a single word. The block just happened to coincide with my oldest son's nervous breakdown and the onset of severe depression. At that time, as I came close to going broke (after receiving a mid-six figure advance for *The Innocent*), I never once stopped working, never once veered from the discipline of waking up every morning and trying to write. "Trying" being the key word here.

Looking back on those difficult years, I realize I wasn't writing so much as

I was just typing, but the process helped me cope with some very difficult and serious issues in my life. If nothing else, the discipline to write can be a mighty powerful therapy.

Eventually the damn breaks, as it did in my case, and I made a return to good writing and publishing. I'm not making millions by any means, but I make a decent living as a freelance journalist and novelist, and that's all anyone can honestly ask for.

The late great Norman Mailer also understood about the financial ups and downs of being a fulltime writer. But more importantly, he understood about the discipline of biting the nail. He wrote 2,500 new words a day right up until the end when his kidneys failed him. It wasn't the disciple or the talent or the mind that gave out, it was the 84 year old body. I'm told he died with a smile on his face. Not the kind of smile that accompanies peace of mind, sedated painlessness, or "going to the bright light." But the kind of smile that only a disciplined writer can wear; the sly grin that means you're about to embark on a brand new adventure, and that you can't wait to write about it.

—*2009*

New Media Love

It's ten o'clock on a cold Sunday night.

I sit at my desk inside my bedroom, eyes glued to a glowing laptop. I pop the cap on a bottle of beer, reach out with my hands, settle them gently on the laptop keyboard, give myself over to the addiction: the incessant need to check my email (AOL and Yahoo); my Facebook updates; my Twitter followers; my Myspace comments . . .

This is the way I rise and fall with each and every day. By updating my life; by being updated by hundreds of other lives. It's also the way I spend a whole lot of hours in between morning and night. Emailing, updating, following, creating, recreating . . . by feeding the bitch.

What happens when I can't sleep?

I check my email.

What did Mailer call the Internet? A bigger waste of time than masturbation.

I'm startled when my cell phone vibrates on the desktop.

I pick it up, glance at the caller ID. I recognize the name. It's a new name, freshly added to my contacts just 48 hours ago. Let's call her A because that's the first letter of her real name. We met online a week or so ago. Cupid.com I believe it was, although it could have been Plentyoffish.com or Match.com. I belong to them all. Keep on casting your profile into the cyber pond and eventually someone will take the bait. Someone beautiful, smart and employed. A woman who is between 5'-0" and 5'-8" and of average to athletic build. A non-smoker, a social drinker who decidedly does not want children. A woman who enjoys quiet dinners and travel and live bands. A woman between the ages of 34 and 44 who is divorced (not separated) or just plain single. A woman of good humor and free of neurosis.

The phone vibrates in my hand.

It feels sort of good vibrating against the skin on my hand.

For a split second I consider punching Ignore. I'm not much in the mood to talk. I'm not much in the mood to talk on the phone, ever.

I answer the phone.

"This a bad time?"

I sip my beer, sit back in my desk chair. On Facebook, my ex-girlfriend (we'll call her S), has tagged me in a picture snapped when we were still in college.

"Just getting ready for bed," I say half-heartedly. In the Facebook photo, I'm sitting on a couch beside the lovely blonde S. We look incredibly young and hopeful.

My new friend A breaks me out of my spell. She doesn't ask, but tells me to hang on while she heads up to her bedroom.

I obey. What choice do I have? I can either hang on or hang up. Over the phone I hear a half-hearted goodnight to A's live-in mother, then the sound of feet climbing the stair-treads, followed by a check on her six year old son in his bedroom.

"Go to sleep, baby. Night night."

The phone pressed up against my ear, I hear bare feet shuffling on carpet. In my head I picture a narrow hallway inside a cookie-cutter split-level. I hear a door close, and a distinct metal against metal latching noise. I know without having to ask that A's now locked and loaded behind her bedroom door. I'm wondering why she just didn't lock herself in for the night and then call me. Maybe she had something to prove to her mother. Maybe she's acting

on impulse. Maybe she's a bit crazy.
Maybe it's me who's crazy. Maybe I should
not have answered the phone in the first
place.

At the same time, I'm picturing the
forty-something woman whose photo ID
I've memorized from the computer. The
dark short hair, the even darker eyes, the
slightly crooked but attractive smile.

I wait for her to say something.

"How was your weekend?"

"This is Albany, remember?"

What I really want to tell her is that
I tried to kill myself with an overdose of
booze and painkillers. But that would be
stretching the truth a teensy-weensy bit.
The booze and painkillers part is all true.
It's just that the actual act of suicide never
entered into my head. Not once. Not really.

On Twitter, a Florida woman posts a
story about an alligator that ate her puppy
dog.

Some A and I back-story: after weeks of cat-and-mouse online conversation, we met face to face for the first time just a few days ago. We "got acquainted" by sharing a cocktail or two and a conversation that transpired more like a job interview. Where did you grow up? Where'd you go to school? How many kids you got? You like your work? Why'd you get divorced? We covered our combined 80 years in the span of a half hour. We covered all the high and low lights. Everything that is, but the truths we decided to leave out. That's the beauty of online dating. You get to edit your life at will.

She's not saying much. But I do hear the rustle of clothing and I know she's getting undressed.

Interesting.

I take another sip of beer. I get new mail on AOL. A note from my band-mate

Davey. Practice on Tuesday and a new show booked for March 13th.

"What's happening?" I say.

"Getting more comfortable," she says.

A drawer opens and closes. More rustling. The abrupt coil-like sound of a body lying back on a mattress; a bed board gently hitting the sheetrock wall. But now instead of background noise, I make out breathing. Heavy, rhythmic breathing gradually picking up speed.

"You . . . alone?"

"Uh huh," I say. I ask what she's doing, even though by now it's pretty obvious.

"You gotta ask," she says like a question

Oh goody, I think. I'm gonna rock out with my cock out.

But a surprising thing happens to me then. A wave of indifference washes over me. What the fuck? I should be honored. I should be into the spontaneity of it all. I'm lucky to have met such a nice woman. Nice, as in a woman who cares enough to share herself with me, even if it is over a cell phone; even if what she's doing is a little out-of-the-Betty-Crocker-norm.

"This is a nice surprise," I say. I'm not sure if I sound sincere enough. But just to make myself sound more sincere, I attempt to play along.

I begin to ask her all the standard questions. What kind of underwear she likes to wear; is she completely shaved; is she into threesomes . . .

"What would we do with another girl?" she muses.

I feel stupid.

I ain't rockin' out and my cock ain't out.

More moaning follows which culminates with a cry and what is obviously a pillow pressed over her face.

You don't want to wake the kid.

Silence ensues.

The silence grows more awkward by the second.

Dead silence.

Politely she asks me if I finished and I have no choice but to lie.

"Sure . . . Great."

"Maybe we can have dinner this week," she says, "and get some of the real thing."

The real thing. I'm not sure I remember the real thing.

But A sounds satisfied and hopeful. Optimistic even. Welcome to the new world order. Facebook, Twitter, phone sex, email sex, text sex. Entire relationships conducted over cellular waves and cyberspace. Why even meet in person. Dig the new media love.

"Yeah," I say, "I'll call you tomorrow."

But it's a lie.

She says goodnight, hangs up. If we were sharing a bed, this would be the part where she rolls over onto her side and I roll over onto mine, our backs facing one another like the reconstruction of the Berlin Wall. In the middle, barbed wired no man's land.

The cell is still hot in my hand.

I make a decision then and there.

I punch contacts.

I find her name and number.

I thumb Options.

I punch Erase.

No more A.

I put the phone down, stare at the computer screen, at the AOL news.

Vincent Zandri

Somewhere in New Orleans, a
Muslim man has beheaded his wife.

I wonder what's gotten into me? But
then I quickly realize that the problem is
not what's gotten into me so much as
what hasn't got out.

It's possible I'm still holding the
torch for my wife.

No, allow me to rephrase for the
sake of accuracy.

It's possible I still love my ex-wife, ex
being the key prefix here, since I just can't
get used to the concept. Even three and a
half years after our official split. Or is it
that I'm in love with the idea of my ex-
wife; the romance we once shared; the
good times; the adventure. Interesting how
all the bad—and there was a lot of it—
never enters the picture.

Christ, maybe I should just get the
hell over it already.

I steal another sip of beer, check the clock.

10:20PM

I pick the phone back up, hit the speed-dial that will connect me to my Ex.

Let's call her L.

She answers wearily, if not groggily.

"I wake you up?"

"You have to ask?"

I feel a strange sensation just hearing her deep voice, knowing that her prone body is lying under the covers, the long smooth dark hair draping the pillow, big brown eyes half open, half closed, her thick lips touching the mouthpiece to the phone that connects to my own and my own lips.

Not so long ago I used to spoon into that body . . . that real human flesh body. I know how her skin smells after a shower. I know how her hair feels in my fingers. I remember how her lips feel against mine. I know the sound of her breathing when she slips into a deep sleep. I remember it all and I relive it often. Especially at night.

Only problem is, I'm no longer sure what's real and what's made up? Where does reality stop and fantasy take over?

I feel my heart skip a beat.

"Can I come over?"

She exhales, "Pleeeaaasseee."

I feel my throat constrict, my pulse elevate. I feel the onslaught of panic. Why the hell did I have to go and ask her that?

"Sorry," I say. "I'm sorry . . . Good night."

"Good night."

I go to tell her I love her, but she's already hung up. The line is dead. I know she wouldn't return the love anyway. Not at this point. But it still feels good to say it now and again.

I love you.

I love the idea of you.

I love the made up memory of you . . . of a past we never really shared.

I set the phone back down on the desk, get undressed, slip into bed.

I keep my eyes open, peer out at the darkness.

The infinite, absolute darkness.

I grow weak.

I close my eyes.

I see nothing.

I grow weaker.

In the morning I will get on with my life.

For now I close my eyes, wait for sleep.

Wait for nothing . . .

—2009

Breakdown

I find him laid out face-first on the floor of the garage. He's banging his forehead against the concrete floor, punching it with tight fists. I can hear the screaming coming from all the way across the apartment complex common. The sounds of his rants are like knives piercing my sternum. He wants to be free of the dreaded weight. He wants out of life.

To witness the nervous breakdown of your own child is no different than watching cancer devour a young body. Like cancer, depression is a powerful disease that can render even the strongest of parents paralyzed. Maybe this isn't my first encounter with his depression-like symptoms, but it is the first encounter with a clinical breakdown.

It is not the stuff for the faint of heart.

When a child like my son Jack suffers a nervous breakdown, it's as if he has become possessed. The violence is a traumatic thing to experience, a frightening scene to witness. He issues guttural screams. He claws at himself, tears at his clothing. He punches the wall full-force, enough to break skin and bone. But he will not feel the pain so much as he will welcome it, covet it, the same way an addict lusts for a drug. This is not Jack lashing out. This is Jack hurting himself. Rather, by hurting himself he is trying to cauterize the deeper pain that has consumed his soul. This is as close as Jack will get to harming himself, without actually committing suicide.

By breakdown's end, the boy is spent.

He is soaked through with sweat;
face and chest moist from tears, saliva
and snot. Dark hair is mussed and
matted. Hands and knees are encrusted
with dirt from the garage floor, some of the
cinders having cut into his skin. He is cut
and bleeding in more than a few places.
It's possible he's broken a finger; maybe a
pulled muscle. His exhaustion is so
profound, he wraps his arm around my
shoulder allowing me to support most of
his weight for the journey from the rented
garage to our terrace apartment.

On the walk across the common, his
head will hang low, chin against chest. Big
tears fall, but the sobs more quiet now.
Voice will be a hoarse whisper.

"I'm sick," he will mutter. "I'm sick."

It's all I can do to hold back my own
tears as I get him through the back door
and onto the couch.

What to do next?

I don't know what to do next. I've never before experienced the breakdown of my child. All I do know is that my pulse pounds, mouth is dry, hands tremble. I need a drink.

Looking at Jack laid out on the couch, eyelids at half-mast, I consider dialing 911. But I fear the move will absolve me of all control. In every "Cuckoo's Nest" sense of the word, I picture the nuthouse. I see straightjackets, injections, big powerful men dressed all in white who instead toss Jack into a rubber room, bolt the door behind him.

Not over my dead body.

I decide to do something totally out of character: I call his mother, seek out her help.

Once more I hold back tears when I tell her, "I can't handle it."

My ex-wife insists he needs a hospital. That she knows what he's going through; that she too had a breakdown not long after our separation which led to months of rehab and a strong medicine which she will ingest for the rest of her life. In the end, her bipolar condition is what led the courts to hand over custody of my two boys to me.

Since then I have tried to play Mr. Mom and Mr. Dad, but looking at my son sprawled out on the couch I feel a failure. My ex, however is willing to do what she can. She's going to place a call to her doc at the Four Winds Psychiatric facility in Saratoga. The doc will in turn call me in order to get a better idea of Jack's symptoms.

I await the call.

When the doc calls I am no longer able to hold back my emotions. The flood gates open. It's some time before I can get my message across.

"My son is sick," I tell him, reiterating Jack's words precisely. "I don't know what to do."

Doc tells me to calm down. That if I fear for Jack's life; for my own life, to immediately get him to the emergency room. I tell him that it's not necessary. I trust my son, even in this condition. I trust in him; trust that he will not do anything to harm himself or me or his little brother.

Then comes the question: Do I have guns in the house? If so, get rid of them. Get rid of anything you might constitute as a dangerous weapon. Hunting knives, ropes, darts, razor blades.

"Ditch the bottle of Tylenol," the doc says. "An overdose can be lethal."

"I prefer Ibuprofen," I tell him.

"Excellent," he says.

He wants to see Jack first thing in the morning, start him on medication. No more school for a while, no more friends or activities. "Keep a close watch on him. Let him sleep if he wants to sleep. Above all, don't excite him."

He hangs up.

I feel drained.

Drained, stomped on, gutted, bled out, crushed . . .

I pop a beer, drink down half of it on one swallow. The alcohol goes right to the sweet spot in my brain, tempers my despair, my anxiety. I stare at Jack on the couch. He's fetal, sleeping like a baby. I remember him as a baby, like it was yesterday. I remember changing his diapers, holding him against me, tossing him in the air, hearing him laugh. The boy passed out on the couch I do not recognize.

What follows over a period of 24 hours is a series of tests and consultations with psychiatrists and psychologists. Jack is placed on anti-anxiety/anti-depression medication. While admittance to a hospital is once more discussed, it is argued by the professionals that to lump Jack in with persons suffering from schizophrenia and psychosis would be a grave mistake. At this stage of the game, that is. This news comes as a relief, although I'm not entirely sure if the relief is for me or for him (I dread the thought of visiting my son in a psychiatric hospital).

Steps must be taken in order to get at the root of the depression. Initially the steps are simple and practical.

Do I possess firearms?

There's that question again.

If so, I must remove them from the premises. There's the answer once again provided for me. Does Jack appear

suicidal? Does he speak of hurting anyone besides himself? Do I fear for my own wellbeing when in his presence?
All the same questions that I fielded during my initial phone conversation the previous evening.

As necessary as the question are, they are disturbing.

I am a gun owner. But I don't fear that Jack is about to use them on me or anyone else, least of all himself. But of course, this is exactly the attitude that will get someone killed. The guns will be removed this afternoon, I assure the doc.

It will be decided that while Jack takes a break from school he is to begin a series of therapy sessions with his psychologist. These will occur three times a week for an hour at a time. The sessions begin the very next day.

His mother and I are called in first to discuss Jack's childhood. Was there fighting around him?

Yes, that's why we divorced.

Did he have tantrums?

Yes, major ones, lasted for hours at a time.

Did he exhibit signs of obsession and/or compulsion?

Yes. For instance, if you didn't tie his shoes perfectly, he'd go into a kind of seizure.

Later, as a pre-teen, he would not leave his bedroom without knocking five times on the wall.

How did he take your divorce?

Not well. He lashed out at his mother. Etc, etc., etc.

By the end of this first fact-finding session I am again crushed, bled out, drained. I am convinced that this boy's problem rests with me and me alone. I am at fault for his breakdown. The way I've raised him is the problem. My ex-wife and I—all the fighting: it is the root cause of Jack's depression.

But then the doctor asks about my family history and a different story emerges altogether. My ex-wife's side has two documented suicides and several more of depression and bipolar syndrome. My ex-wife herself is bipolar. As for my side, it's no better.

I immediately recall a story my dad told me about his own early teenage years. How one afternoon he came home from school and without warning found himself clutching at the driveway, convinced he was about to climb up on the roof, toss himself off. A nervous breakdown followed. He was later diagnosed with depression, at a time when depression was considered shameful. Those persons afflicted with it were to be hidden, kept out of sight of the "normal" people.

My father would go on to beat his depression to become a successful business owner. Yet he would still suffer two more breakdowns. Because the depression never really leaves you. It disappears, goes into a kind of remission. You can't fight genetics. One day he would tell me of my great grandfather who committed suicide at the dinner table—by cutting his own neck with a straight razor in front of the whole family.

The doctor looks at my ex-wife and I, raises his right hand up and down and up again.

"This depression is genetic in nature," he says. "And it is weaving its way in and out of your bloodline."

Bloodline.

Sitting there inside that office I
suddenly regret having had children.
It is not a good thought.

This is not so good either: Jack is
not genetically blessed and it breaks my
heart.

But this is the modern world.
Medicine and therapies are available now
that can afford Jack a "normal" life. So the
doc encourages.

Nor is the stigma of depression an
issue.

I have no problem writing about it.
It is my own therapy to write about it. If
only I could step inside my son's mind,
observe the grinding wheels and gears,
observe the monster hidden behind them.
I might understand more, be able to better
write about it.

But no matter how close I am to my
child, I am an outsider looking in. I am on

my knees looking down into the pit. There is nothing but cold darkness.

The news is not all bad.

In one week's time, Jack makes his first advance. He cracks a smile.
I'm not entirely sure what provokes it.
Something I say or his little brother says.
Maybe something Kramer spits on a "Seinfeld" rerun.
A simple smile. A grin really.

It's not a whole lot. You might not give it a second thought under any other circumstance. Anything normal that is. But for me, that smile represents hope. It is the future and it is possibility. It warms my soul like mother's milk.

I know that we have a long road ahead. There will be more breakdowns. But perhaps the next time it happens, Jack will be ready for it. When it does, I will be there to carry his weight.

—2009

Three Hearts Beat as One

L and I talked a bit tonight . . .
Correction, we've talked a lot since the
first blog post a few days ago. It seems to
have created a bit of a stir. From Mexico to
NYC to Los Angeles to Bulgaria and in
between, the reactions poured in. Okay,
trickled in, but it's still pretty cool how
this blog-thingy works.

Instant gratification.

Said reactions and commentary
culminated with a call to me from L while I
was grabbing a beer at a favorite dive after
a Blisterz rehearsal.

"Who . . . is . . . L?" she demanded.

"You gotta ask?" I said about the
clamor. "Helloooo?"

I'd been snagged, fair and double
square.

The truth: a mutual friend had alerted L to what was happening via a Facebook message. Thank God for Facebook. "Oh my," is how said mutual friend put it.

Oh my, indeed.

But L was and is, in a word, cool about it.

L is into it!

For once, we are in total agreement. My guess is that she is looking for a way to get me back. Which is nice, but I'm not that easy. Okay, yes I am . . . and I'm a big fat liar. I'm not sure she wants me back. Or perhaps it's the other way around. Although I would never admit to this in public. Or maybe I just did.

But L did bring up a startling suggestion.

Perhaps we should write a book together . . . about love and heartbreak

and reunion. I think it should be a crime
novel. Our split . . . It was a crime.

Oh, and have I mentioned L invited
me over to her house last night?

But only to talk . . .

To talk, damnit!

No bootie calls!!!

We talked.

I wanted more.

I always want more.

She was wearing a sheer blouse and
low cut sweat pants . . . Hang-out-who-
care clothes.

She looked ravishing.

She sat on her bed. I lay beside her.
We were breathing in and exhaling our
combined air, stirring to mutual
heartbeats.

Moments later, I listened to the
sound of my daughter's breathing through
her bedroom door. I sensed her heart
pumping blood through veins and

capillaries. An integrated network of life. A body of cells, blood and oxygen. A body that is as much my own as it is L's.

Moments after that, I left, wondering how long my heart has to beat . . . Without L . . . Without our baby.

I wonder still.

(To be continued . . .)

—2009

The Dead Giveaway

I'm barely through the front door of the house (*her* house) when she grabs hold of my arm, pulls me into the unlit bedroom that adjoins the vestibule and the bathroom. Without a word, she takes hold of my wrist, guides my right hand down into the front of her jeans.

The jeans are already unbuttoned.

Like a snake through wet grass, I slide in easily. She must have unbuttoned the jeans before I came through the door. She must have unbuttoned them knowing I would do this; knowing I would want to do this.

"Make me cum," L whispers, wet lips pressed against my lobe.

She's not wearing underwear, so I feel her moist, soft place. I feel it on my fingers, my fingers inching and moving in and over and around and in. It's a nice, soft, warm, neatly trimmed place.

I work slow but fast; gentle but rough, her long black hair splashing against my face.

She kisses my neck with those lips I remember, breathes in and out hard and rapid, braces herself with her arms balanced on my shoulders, hands pressed against the back of my head.

It happens.

She shudders, bites my neck.

Coming from the bathroom beside the bedroom, the splash of bathtub water.

And a voice.

"Mommy."

"Coming sweety," she says.

"Yes you are," I whisper.

She pulls my hand out, buttons up, exits the bedroom for the bathroom.

"Time to wash your hair, my love."

Later I walk alone in the deep night.

I still smell her on my fingers even though I have washed.

When I smell L, I picture her face— the thick lips, the small nose, the dark eyes. I feel my stomach go tight, my throat closes up. On the rare occasion this happens, it's not unusual for my eyes to tear up. When I smell her scent I am reminded of loss. Loss washes over me like a waterfall of blood and tears. It's the tangible things I miss: the scent, the feel, the touch, the lips on a neck, the fingers on her moist sex, her mouth on my body. It's the chemical properties of us that I miss. The physical us. Us together as a whole. The tenderness of us.

Or maybe tenderness never entered the "us" equation.

I try to put "us" of my mind. But no soap in the world, no matter how expensive, can remove that scent.

I make a pit-stop at my local for a quick beer.

The place is dead. Empty. But I catch the eyes of a young woman seated on the opposite end of the horseshoe bar. "Young woman" is a stretch. The girl is maybe 21, 22 at most. A couple years older than my oldest son. Long brunette hair, dark eyes, smooth skin. Knock out, drop-dead-gorgeous.

I've seen her around. I sit next to her.

She smiles that slow-mo, milky eyed smile that tells me she's had a few already.

"You're sexy for an old guy," she says with a giggle.

I feel my 44 year old face go redder than Johnny Walker. I try to respond, but my mouth is clamped shut.

She leans into me, pert young breasts nearly pressing up against me.

"I'd fuck you," she whispers. "Totally."

I laugh. I laugh because my built-in auto-response mechanism appears to have malfunctioned. I laugh, like an ass, in the face of this beautiful girl. Yeah, I want to fuck her. You betcha. But I also want to crawl under a bar stool and disappear.

I'm a total choke.

But here we are seated next to one another at an otherwise empty bar. She, a ravishing 21 or 22 and me, a useless 44. The resulting heavy silence turns into senseless and stupid chit-chat that lasts for the length of one beer.

Bored, beautiful girl gets up and leaves.

The bartender, a young muscle-bound man not much older than she is, approaches me. He tosses me a glance that could cut a rattlesnake in two at thirty paces.

"Nice work, Chief," he says.

The next morning, I buy two large coffees, bring them with me back to the house (*her* house).

L is still in her pajamas. She's moving furniture around. A chair here; a sofa there; a desk up against the far wall. It's what she does every Sunday morning. So I recall. This obsession with moving the furniture around . . . it's not like she's trying to rearrange the living room so much as trying to rearrange her life.

I smell her scent inside the house. It enters my mouth and nasal passages, jump starts my senses like hot volts to the naked wire.

I say "Hello," set the coffees on the coffee table.

I ask about the little one. The little one is in the bedroom playing.

"Nicely," she says, before issuing me a wave of the hand; before guiding me into her bedroom, and finally the bathroom.

She unbuckles my belt, unbuttons my jeans. She pulls down her bottoms, lets them fall to her ankles, turns to face the sink and the medicine cabinet mirror. She reaches under, guides me into her.

It takes all of three minutes, the bathroom door slightly ajar so that she can listen for the child.

Later, after washing, we sit at the table, drinking tepid coffee.

I smell her scent on my hands mixed with the rosy smell of pricey hand soap.

I feel the tightness in my stomach, the closing up of my throat.

"That was nice," I say. "The past couple of times . . . It's been nice."

She looks up at me quick—wide, dead-giveaway-eyes.

"Don't get carried away," she says, out the corner of her mouth.

Tight stomach falls to the linoleum. You can almost hear it go splat.

"Why do you say that?"

She cocks her head, sips her coffee, peers off into a kitchen landscape of modern cooking appliances, junk drawers, rack drying china, cutlery and spilling over garbage cans.

"It's just fucking," she says. "And that's all."

—2009

Pieces of Mind

5 Things I Learned while Writing *Moonlight Falls*: An interview by Sia McKye

It's my pleasure to welcome Noir Thriller author, Vincent Zandri, back to Over Coffee. He's one of my favorite people who aside from writing some fabulous thrillers, plays in a band.

He is a drummer in the Albany-based punk band The Blisterz. What can I say; I've always had a weakness for smart witty men who play music. :-)

Vin, like many authors today, has to juggle life as a single father of three, with working full time. As a photojournalist, he has traveled extensively to Russia, Italy, China,

Africa, Turkey, Greece, England, France, and more.

In addition to an award-winning novelist, Zandri is also a freelance essayist and writes for various global publications. Vincent currently divides his time between New York and Europe.

I appreciate his drive and ambition to write despite the various changes in the publishing market. Changes we've all seen—whether we are readers or fellow writers. Instead of letting setbacks or rejections stop him he's wisely taken the time to learn lessons along the way and apply them.

He agreed to share some of those lessons here. Your thoughts on his lessons are welcomed.

Many things were learned during the five on-again, off-again years while I was writing my new noir, thriller, *Moonlight Falls*, the least of which, is that initial publishing success can be fading. Back in 1999, when my first commercial thriller, *The Innocent* (originally titled, *As Catch Can)*, was first published in hardcover by Delacorte, I assumed that I had found a permanent literary home for the rest of my life, and that the next stop in my green career was the Pulitzer Prize. But when Delacorte merged with another publisher, many of its authors were quickly transferred elsewhere and from there, kindly shown the door. For me, it was back to square one.

But despite the trial and tribulations of a commercial publishing world that has been described as "perilous," I was nonetheless able to adhere to a program of good, solid writing, day in and day out. That alone became my shield against a volatile publishing business. That alone was my guiding force in a short literary life that had seen great ups and that now, was realizing a very deep, seemingly bottomless pit.

Still I trudged on through a period of several years where I did not publish a single book, but instead concentrated on the writing of several manuscripts, not the least of which, became *Moonlight Falls*.

Here are five things I learned about myself and the world around me during that time.

- *Nothing replaces rock solid writing, research and rewriting.* Or, the three R's, if you will. Even though I might have quit the business altogether and moved on to something less volatile than the writing and publishing life, I still adhered to a rigorous writing program day in and day out, even when there was no money coming in. I chose this path because in the back of my head, I always knew that the novel would one day be published. Not self-published, mind you, but published in the traditional format. Which leads me to . . .

- *Never lose your faith in yourself and your ability, even in the face of domestic non-tranquility.* Things around the house during my, let's call them "wilderness years," were not very happy. I'd just married my second wife, Laura, whom I believed was my soul mate. We came together at a time when things were great. I was on top of the world as a writer and we were traveling the world. But then, when things got hard. I retreated back into my shell and nearly lost all confidence in my ability to write a great story. But curiously, and sadly, as Laura and I began to break up, I regained my confidence. Which leads me to . . .

- *Don't quit the day job.* Or in my case, don't give up the freelance writing and journalism because you're suddenly under the impression you're the next Norman Mailer. What you must constantly remind yourself is that even a world renowned writer like Mailer was broke half the time. When I published *The Innocent* and the follow up, *Godchild*, I assumed I'd never have to write another stitch of journalism again; that I could place all my literary eggs into one basket. Turns out, had I kept my foot in the freelance writing door, I might have saved my marriage and my home by maintaining at least a semblance of income. Luckily, I was able to make a return to journalism but only after the domestic damage was done. Which leads me to . . .

- *Learn to weather the storms and know when to move on with your life.* Said another way, learn how to swallow your pride. It's a tough thing losing everything you have worked so hard for in life, from your publisher to your wife to your home. But to have it all happen at once, well, that's enough to break even the strongest man for good. But this is the life we live as writers and novelists. This is the life we have chosen. While in many ways I would stop at nothing to have my wife back, I know I am powerless to do anything about it other than write the best I can, and do so consistently and without prejudice; without concern for what the publishing market is currently bearing. Which leads me to . . .

- *The publishing market is undergoing severe and rapid change.* Traditional commercial publishers are dying. Don't let them tell you otherwise. What's replacing them are electronically based, independent houses that although utilizing the traditional publishing model of accepting a manuscript based upon its merits as a work of art, now publish the manuscripts in both electronic and POD format. Yes, the independent bookstores will hate you for it, and even turn up their

Vincent Zandri

noses at you. But 90% of all book buyers are making their purchases online. Many of them are doing so via Kindle, I-Phone, BlackBerry, and other electronic means.

It's the new world publishing model of social media, virtual tours, book trailers, blog talk radio, mommy blogs, etc., and it is here to stay. More than likely, it will give over to an influx of self-published material over the next few years, while big agent firms and big publishers die off.

—2010

Pieces of Mind

An Interview by Literarily Speaking

Thank you for this interview, Vincent. Your book, *The Remains*, has just been released on Kindle, then the trade paperback will be released this fall. How do you feel about having your book in this medium first and paperback later?

Well, to be more precise, *The Remains* is released first as an E-Book, which means it will be available on Kindle, I-pod, Smashwords, Nook, and just about any electronic device known to man and robot. The fact that it will be released first as an E-Book and later as paper makes perfect sense to me, for two reasons. The New York City big publishers I used to publish with release their books in just the opposite order, which tells me Stone House is doing something right. The old big houses have an antiquated system which still relies on a small percentage of sales revenues going to the author. They also are tied into that terrible system of allowing bookstores the option of returning books. I simply never understood the logic or the business model. By being released as an E-Book first, there is a strong likelihood *The Remains* will hit the Number One spot on Amazon or at least come close. That alone will fuel a very good print run later on down the line. I suppose for a more complete answer you would have to speak with my publisher and agent, but what I've told you comes pretty close to the mark.

Whose idea was it to do it this way and what is their strategy?

Again, you'd have to refer to the publisher. But like I just answered, bestselling electronic sales will fuel an excellent print run later on down the line. And since the printing method will be POD, it will be a responsible print run with zero returns. This new method of publishing also allows me a huge percentage of sales that I would have only dreamt about with the NYC Biggies. Finally, *The Remains* will be in print and available as an E-Book forever and ever. It will be the gift that keeps on giving. Welcome to the new world publishing order.

Do you think people are going to be receptive to reading your book on an e-reader rather than paper?

Initially some will, and some won't. People like my parents and their generation, might prefer to wait until the novel is available in paper. Some people like myself, who own an extensive library, will prefer to wait until it comes out on paper. But those who live and die by their Kindles and IPods, they will be more than receptive. In fact, I'm frantically working on another novel, *The Concrete Pearl*, which will be a new series, in order to help feed their habit. But of course, first Stone House has to read and decide whether or not to take it on. By the way, I'm told that Kindle books and the like are outselling paper books by a margin of 6-1!

What's your experience with ebooks? Do you own an e-reader and, if so, have you ever read an ebook? If not, have you read one through your computer? Do you know anyone with an e-reader?

Well, I own a Kindle on my computer and I've downloaded the reader to my Blackberry. I've yet to read a book on Kindle, but as a journalist I fly to

Europe and other destinations fairly often. Now, instead of packing six pounds worth of books, I'll use my reader. When I get back, if I want to order those same books in hard or soft cover for my library, I will do so. Oh, and also, lots of indie publishers, Like R.J. Buckley for instance, who published my recent noir thriller, *Moonlight Falls* on Kindle and as a trade paperback, now forward galley proofs as electronic PDFs. So in that sense, I have already read my first novel in electronic format.

Regardless of which format they choose to read your new book, I'm sure it's going to be another Vincent Zandri winner. How is it different from your first book, *Moonlight Falls*? Everyone I have talked to fell in love with that one!

In technical terms, *Moonlight Falls* is my first noir thriller in a while. The first two, *As Catch Can* and *Godchild*, were published by Dell, and quickly made unavailable even after a mid-six-figure advance and awesome reviews like "Brilliant . . ." by the *New York Post* and "The most arresting first crime novel to break into print this season," by the *Boston Herald.* In fact those two books are now considered noir classics in some circles and were recently included in an extensive history of noir written by Detroit author and noir critic, Heath Lowrance.

As for the difference between *The Remains* and *Moonlight Falls? The Remains* features a very strong, female protagonist, painter and painting teacher, caught up in a nightmarish situation. She's simply different from Richard Moonlight in that she's a little more controlled. She's even got a real job! But much like Richard Moonlight, some of the life-and-death problems that stem from

her past have now come back to haunt
her. Or, in this case, come back to literally
kill her. While *Moonlight Falls* is not
necessarily a novel for everyone, due to its
subject matter, style, and language *The
Remains* is a far more accessible
mainstream read for all sort of readers,
ages and tastes. It's still dark, still pile-
driver plotted, still noir, but no one's doing
heroin in this one, if you get my drift. PG
as opposed to R-rated.

**I love (as you know!) the haunted
looking house on the cover. Why is the
house significant?**

That's the place where my
protagonist Rebecca Underhill and her late
twin sister Molly, were abducted, tortured
and kept in a basement 30 years ago by a
murderer and serial rapist named Joseph
William Whalen. Having been in prison all
these years, Joseph is back on the streets
and he once more wants to spend a little

quality time with his one surviving girl. The image and the novel were inspired by the nightmares we've all had at one time or another in which you find yourself alone inside an abandoned house or building.

If you could compare your book to a movie, which one would that be?

Think *Along Came a Spider* meets *The Blair Witch Project*!

Thank you so much for this interview, Vincent. Do you have any final words?

Final words? Is my computer about to explode in my face? Ha!!! LOL.

—2010

The Case of an Autistic Savant!

Lots of interviewers ask me if I base my characters on real people. And the answer is yes and no. While I always write about real people and real events, I'm pretty good at twisting around the truth to suit my purposes. In the case of *The Remains*, my newest thriller, I borrowed a real life character from my childhood by the name of Francis Scaramuzzi.

Francis worked in my high school, The Albany Academy, which at the time was a military themed, country day prep school. He was a simple man. What we then called mentally challenged. A sweet, short, portly character who seemed more boy than man, despite his middle age, Francis loved the school and the boys who attended it. He worked in the cafeteria, or what was called, The Buttery, and on occasion he'd hand out towels to the boys on their way out of the showers after athletics. Often, at the end of the day, I'd see Francis waiting at the bus stop on the corner, standing anxiously, wool cap pulled over his head, over-sized jeans yanked way up over his belly, a paper shopping bag in his hand.

I couldn't help but wonder where he lived, and what his home was like. If he lived alone or if he lived with relatives or friends. But it wasn't until many years later, when Francis was in ill health and close to death, that it was discovered he spent many of his nights painting. His painting contained brilliant colors and crafty illustrations and very much reminded the school's art prof of Grandma Moses in theme, tone and delivery. Many of these paintings were sold on Francis's behalf and for a short time, he enjoyed some local fame and notoriety from the local Albany, New York art scene.

Francis, it was discovered, wasn't a simple mentally challenged man so much as he was a gifted painter. A savant. He was the real thing and more.

When I set out to write *The Remains*, I wanted to make the fascinating Francis a central character and a kind of hero. So I created an autism for him, and made him into a savant who, like the real man, has a terrific gift for painting. In the story, his paintings send messages to the book's central character, Rebecca Underhill, and warning her about a man who has been released from prison and who is now out to get her.

Thanks Francis, wherever you are. For me you are both real and imagined. Your memory is not lost with the ages but lives on in your paintings and your humble character, which now is immortalized in, *The Remains.*

—*2010*

The Prodigal Thriller Writer

A lot can change in six months. In just one week I'll receive a statement from my agent which she will receive from one of my two traditionally-based indie publishers regarding sales for *Moonlight Falls*.

I'm not sure what to expect. But I do anticipate good news since "Moonlight" has been that company's bestseller every month since it came out in December 2009. It also spent a brief time as an Amazon.com bestseller.

Prior to six months ago, I was simply a working stiff freelance journalist who was spending lots of time traveling abroad looking for stories to report or blog about. When news came of an acceptance on *Moonlight Falls* from a very small publisher, me and my agent didn't have any high expectations for it. We merely giggled and agreed that we'd have a nice looking book to sell to my friends, fans and family. But since that time, I've contracted with a larger indie publisher who has already put out my newest thriller, *The Remains*, in E-Book and Kindle. It will also be out in trade paperback in November. The audio rights have sold and a very good bookstore distribution agreement has ensued. And who would have *thunk* it, but *The Remains* is an Amazon bestseller right out of the gate, and as of last night was listed as an Amazon "Hot New Release" in "Hard Boiled" Kindle.

In the wake of that initial success, I've just signed a contract for both the republication of my 1999 thriller, *As Catch Can*, and my new thriller series, *The Concrete Pearl*, to a new imprint largely

started for me and a few other novelists
and writers.

To what do I attribute the new found
success? I'm not sure, other than perhaps
my timing is right. Listen, prior to six
months ago, I assumed there might not be
a market for my fiction. That, like the
great noir novelist before me, Jim
Crumley, I might be relegated to pretty
much a cult following. And I was fine with
that, so long as I could publish a small
press effort every few years, pay my bills
and travel while working as a full-time
writer and journalist. But now it turns
out, my audience is expanding like crazy.
Every day it gets bigger.

So, back to the timing thing. Has
the emergence of E-Books and Kindle
helped my efforts? You betcha. Although I
had somewhat of a platform on which to
build thanks to having two critically
acclaimed thrillers published under two

Random House imprints, said platform wasn't all that big anymore, and in fact, was dangerously close to being tossed into the "has been" bucket. But the new electronic publishing model has rapidly changed all that.

Is the on-line publishing world about to become filled up with a whole bunch of crap just because it's easy for independents to get their work out there? Of course it will. But when hasn't there been a whole bunch of crap out there for people to waste their money on? Crap that bleeds off the fingertips of some pretty big perpetual *New York Times* bestsellers?

What makes the new publishing model interesting and exciting (and has big New York sweating under the pits!) is finally, we all have a level playing field in which to compete for unlimited space. *The Remains* is selling better than Patterson, Coben, Parker, LeHane and more in several categories. That's not to say that it's better than what they are writing. It's to say that people who enjoy those authors are getting somewhat of a kick out of my new books too. And even though they are also being released in paper and audio, the electronic versions will be available forever. If this were ten years ago, and I were limited to just the Barnes and Nobles tables of the world, *The Remains* would probably already be heading to the *Remain*der bin. It simply wouldn't have the backing or the support that the mega authors enjoy.

Don't worry about a whole bunch of crap filling up Amazon and other markets. I trust readers to always pick out the cream and leave the crap behind, just like they always have. But with the new publishing model comes the opportunity for formerly forgotten authors like me to reach a massive audience. It will also allow a talented selection of newbies to outsell their mega-heroes.

I'm now the prodigal son returned to a publishing world that's been turned over on its back. And I'm kicking some real ass!!!

Gee, it's good to be back home.

—*2010*

Frank Nash: A Most Inspirational English Teacher

I never set out to be a writer. Back in 1979, when I entered the Second Form in a 200 year old, all boys, military school called, The Albany Academy, I simply wanted to become a rock n' roll star. Like Ringo or Keith Moon, I wanted to play drums in a huge rock band, make a ton of money doing it, get lots of girls, and see the world. While most of the uniformed boys sat attentively in math class, taking copious notes, I drew illustrations of huge drums sets and stared out the window.

All that changed when for the first time, I was introduced to Frank Nash in my second term English lit and writing course. First thing that caught my

attention was the classroom itself. The
Academy was an old building even back
then, having been built in the 1920s.
Made of stone and strong woods, with real
blackboards instead of chalk boards, the
place seemed like a kind of time warp. A
school caught perpetually in the 19th
century instead of one that would see the
21st century in only two more decades.

But Mr. Nash's room had a special
allure to it since it was filled with photos
of famous authors, the most notable for
me, was Ernest Hemingway. The framed
photo was a famous headshot that I would
later learn had been taken by the world
renown photographer, Karsh, in 1957, the
lens having captured the 58 year old
Pulitzer and Nobel Prize winning writer
dressed in a big, bulky, turtleneck
sweater, his Old Man and the Sea style
beard and matching white hair giving him
the look of a sea captain or world explorer,

which of course fit the bill perfectly for since the adventurous Hemingway was all of those things and more.

I recall Mr. Nash entering the classroom on the very first day of school, the weather still warm and bright and summer-like. He was a tall, thin man, who wore cowboy boots and jeans—a casual style which seemed to go against the more conservative wool-suited style of some of the more uptight Academy profs. A decorated war vet, he sat on a bar stool in the front of the class, and he talked with us like we were his bar buddies, not as if we were a bunch of stupid kids. Our first read for the semester was A Farewell to Arms, and when he described the novel to us, he did so in manner that seemed strange. First off, he referred to the author not as Ernest Hemingway, but as "Papa." Was Frank Nash Hemingway's kid? He talked about Papa's writing habits, about his fishing and hunting and travelling, about his eventual suicide by self-inflicted gunshot. He even demonstrated how Papa placed both barrels of the shotgun inside his mouth, pressed them against the soft palate, and how he triggered the hammers with his thumb. I remember looking up at the Karsh photo and trying to imagine the writer's head blown off, and I recall being thoroughly spooked, but somehow excited.

Then, and only then, did Nash crack the book and begin to read that lovely, lush opening about being at war with the dust from the road clinging to the leaves on the trees and each sentence connected to the other with the conjunction "and." Nash loved that opening and as tough and worldly as he seemed, I could see now that it was possible for a hard man to also be a sensitive man of letters.

We talked a lot about Hemingway and war and adventure that first month of school and I came to realize that Frank Nash was an expert on Hemingway. I found myself so immersed in reading "Farewell" and listening to Nash's lectures on writing and Papa, that I never once felt like scribbling a drum set in my notebook or felt the need to fight off boredom by looking out the window. That is, unless Nash was inviting us too.

I listened and I learned and I wrote my first essays on Hemingway. I also wrote my first short story which Nash read aloud in class as an example of promising material. It was a story about spending a grueling Easter Sunday with my family and it was graded with a big fat, red, "A." Nash pulled me aside and he asked me what I wanted to be when I grew up. I told him a rock drummer. And he laughed, and said, "Well, maybe you should write some stories along the way."

When we arrived back at school after the Christmas break, I was excited to see Frank Nash again. It had been a long Christmas break and I was eager to read some more classic novels and to write more stories. But something had changed. Nash was still there, but something had happened to him in the short time that we'd been apart. His hands shook almost uncontrollably, and he seemed out of it. His eyes were glassy and he looked gaunt and pale and sick.

He lasted a few more days that second semester, but then he didn't show up at all. When the Dean of the upper school sent someone to his downtown Albany apartment to check up on the English teacher, they found a reclusive Nash consumed in whiskey. Empty bottles of Jack Daniels were strewn about the living room and the bathtub was full of ice and cans of beer. The shades had been drawn on the windows and aside from stacks and stacks of books, there was only a desk with an old Royal typewriter sitting on top of it. The pile of manuscript pages beside it contained stories about the old Albany Academy. It turned out Frank was writing a biography of the old military school. He was, at the same time, drinking himself to death.

In the Fall of the next year, the Albany Academy was still there, but Frank Nash did not go to it anymore. Eventually he sought out help for his alcoholism and returned to his native Vermont where he lived with fellow veterans, and wrote some of his own stories and poems. When my first big novel *As Catch Can* was published in 1999, my publisher sent him an autographed copy. But I never heard back from him. I wondered if he remembered me at all. I wondered if he read the book and if he had, if he liked it. But then, it wasn't important if he did or didn't. What was important was the fact that for three months, I was lucky enough to be taught by a man who felt as though he was so close to the words of Ernest Hemingway he could refer to him as Papa in every bit of the fatherly sense of the word. To this day, I think of Nash as Papa in the same inspirational manner. Nash altered the course of my young life and because of him I became a writer. I'm lucky to have known him and even more lucky to remember him the way he was when he was teaching and writing and was very happy.

—*2010*

What is Suspense?

A promising young MFA in Writing graduate student asked me if I would answer a few questions for him regarding his academic thesis, which stems around the topic of "suspense." I guess it shouldn't surprise most of you thriller, mystery and noir fans, that not a whole lot of information can be found on the subject in the stuffy, closed-in world of academia.

So here goes.

1. Is there really such a thing as "literary suspense?"

   I'm not entirely sure what "literary suspense" means. Other than it means the precise key ingredient variety of suspense that's found in genre fiction, be it mystery, thriller, romantic-suspense, etc., that can also stand up there with the high-brow, quote "literary" unquote, fiction.

From a personal POV, my first big novel, *As Catch Can*, was bought by Delacorte Press back in 1999 and was considered a "literary thriller." What this means is that I wrote what was then called a "Hitchcockian thriller" that contained both the necessary stuff to satisfy both the readers of genre fiction and literary fiction. In other words, the novel contained lots of conflict, drama, suspense, sex, violence, humor, lies, deceits and deceptions, and all those other things that make a thriller an exciting, can't put it down, read. Chapters were short, and sentences tight and taught, the dialogue as crisp, tough and in some cases, as cryptic as a Hemingway short story. But it also contained vivid imagery (I did my own MFA thesis on "imagery""), the occasional but not over-abused use of metaphor, and an emotional subplot of a man who is up against it all while having recently lost his wife to cancer. Delacorte promoted the books as a literary thriller reminiscent of Hitchcock's *North By Northwest* perhaps to open up the market to both literary fans and genre fans who might be willing to try out a new novel by an MFA grad who was also a rather serious minded freelance journalist.

Even my newest bestseller, *The Remains*, contains all the essential elements of a hard-boiled thriller, while quickly becoming popular with the more literary crowd. Once again, it's also been compared with Hitch's work. It's got pile-driving plotting, short chapters and plenty of action. But the story revolves around a painter and painting as an art. It's also told from the point of view of a female art teacher. Hardly the stuff of tough guy thriller fiction.

So in short, yes, a novel can be considered both literary and suspenseful. Look for both in the best suspense novels that stand the test of time, like The Last Good Kiss, by Jim Crumley and To Have and Have Not by Ernest Hemingway. Look for only the suspense part in novels that will be forgotten in time. No need to list the little buggers here.

2. What are some techniques a writer can use to build tension?

I posed this question on Facebook just a little while ago and each response differed from the other. In general though, most agree that writing short chapters, and short, sharp sentences definitely service to build tension, as opposed to long, flowing, obnoxious, Dickins-like sentences that tend to put you to sleep.

This is personal, but I prefer to work in the first person, especially with an unreliable narrator who cannot be trusted and who might not always be in the right, but who is after something that is inevitably righteous, even if he or she has to break the law in order to find it. Not knowing if you narrator is going to turn out to be the one who actually killed the cat will always make for a riveting read. Check out my critically acclaimed and bestselling noir novel, *Moonlight Falls*, for instance. Again, it was compared to Hitchcock!

Another technique is to put in all

the violence and the action. I
once had a writing teacher at
MFA school who insisted that I
only "imply" violence and action,
not dramatize it on the page. For
reasons beyond my control I
followed his advice all that
semester. But once it was over, I
put all the good stuff back into
my manuscript. He's now long
forgotten as a writer. I'm a
bestseller.

3. Is the role of suspense
different in mysteries than it is
literary fiction?

Suspense is dramatic conflict of
one kind or another and every
good story, literary or not, needs
conflict. Otherwise there's
nothing novel to write about.

Even if you're subject is a plain old orange, you can find suspense: just what is it you're going to find underneath all that skin after you tear into it with your bear, bleeding hands?

You're not going to find much in terms of who-dunnit suspense in literary fiction, but you will find suspense, even if it's a band of orthodox Jews and Romans who band together to crucify an upstart Jewish carpenter.

4. Is suspense a necessary universal component of all fiction, no matter the genre?

Yes. Otherwise it's poetry. There must be a reason for a novel to be written. That reason usually stems from a conflict or the birth of a suspenseful moment. I.E. A man comes home from work to discover his wife has packed up the kids and left him for good; a young woman walks into a coffee shop and believes she sees her former boyfriend. When she confronts him, he denies having ever seen her before; when a young woman begins receiving strange text messages, she starts to believe that the man who abducted she and her twin sister 30 years ago is back. And this time, he wants to kill her (the premise of my novel, *The Remains*).

So there it is. My take on suspense. Right or wrong. But from a very personal point of

view, I prefer not to read
something that doesn't have
suspense in it. It's like eating a
chocolate chip cookie without the
chips. It just falls flat and is
uninteresting. A plain vanilla
cookie with no color, drama or
sweet richness. In a nutshell, if
you haven't worked up a good
sweat after reading something, it
ain't worth it!

—2010

The Fall and the Rise: My Story Bulleted

Here's how I first came to be published commercially in Big NYC:

❖ I wrote a novel called *The Innocent* about a prison warden wrongly accused of aiding and abetting the escape of a convicted cop-killer. It was based on a true story.

❖ I got an agent for the novel. Let's call him Slick.

❖ Slick sold the novel in two weeks in a deal totaling 230,000 clams. I loved Slick and dedicated the novel to him.

- ❖ The acquiring editor was a musician and a pretty smart lit guy who had also first bought Harlan Coben. Let's call him J. We became quick buds.

- ❖ J's only senior in the publishing house was a woman named L. She was the editor-in-chief I guess. She was a sweet lady.

- ❖ My publicist was young woman named V, whom I liked very much. Well, ok, I liked her a lot.

- ❖ There was a buzz about *The Innocent* from the start. *Publishers Weekly* published two pre-pub pieces. A record Japanese deal was struck. DreamWorks was all over the movie rights. Dutch rights sold.

- ❖ I joined a band with J, called StrawDogs, and partied like a rock star. I also partied with V, and well, you know . . . .

- ❖ Then something terrible happened. Talk of a corporate takeover infected the publisher's Times Square office. Suddenly everyone was worried about their jobs. Something new was about to be introduced to the book market as well. EBooks. Bookstore owners were in a panic.

* ❖ Too much time began to pass from contract execution to actual book publication. More than a year. As worries over takeovers and EBooks began to infect the publishing office, interest in *The Innocent* began to wane.

* ❖ J had to change the name of the book to *As Catch Can* because some author in a sister firm had published a book by that title a couple of years before. "As Catch . . . what?" I posed . . .

❖ A year came and went, and
still As Catch Whatever hadn't
been released. But they were
working on it. The cover was
finally completed, but it was
rushed. No one really liked it,
but too much time had
passed, so it was used. It was
an ugly green on top of
illegible letters.

❖ Still, the book was published
to amazing reviews like
"Brilliant," and "The most
arresting crime novel to be
published this year." Maybe
the reviews would aid sales!!!

❖ Borders Books took it off the
shelves after six weeks. Big
Commercial Bookstore Policy!

- ❖ Everyone at the publishing house was worried for their job.

- ❖ No one promoted *Catch*. Not even V.

- ❖ The hostile takeover happened. So did EBooks.

- ❖ *As Catch Can* drowned in Big NYC corporate turmoil.

- ❖ Slick refused to do anything about it when J suggested we take the book to another publisher. Slick didn't care. He'd gotten his money. He was playing the stock market and onto something else.

❖ The new "hostile" publisher
had to take me on, under the
pretense of contractual
obligation. They published my
second novel, *Godchild*, in
mass paperback, shit it out,
and quickly forgot about it.

❖ My editor at the time told me
in confidence, "The publisher
is preventing you from selling
books."

❖ I'd lost all control. My rights
were locked up. My lit career
was not only in a stall, it was
about to crash and burn. All
because of corporate greed.
My life entered into a tailspin .
. .

❖ So what's to be learned here? Just because you land a big deal in NYC does not guarantee you huge success. In fact, it can spell disaster of major proportions. So what's happened to all the major players?

❖ Slick is reputedly running for his life, his office shut down, his AAR status revoked. Keep running Slick . . .

❖ The Editor-in Chief, L, is out of the business (I met her in the lobby of the Bertelsmann Building, her desk lamp in hand, tears streaming down her cheeks. She sweetly kissed me, and uttered, "Good luck." But what she really meant was "Rest in Peace."

❖ J is doing cool things at MTV
with pop culture books. He
couldn't be happier.

❖ I never heard from V again . . .
But sometimes I wonder what
she's up to.

❖ StrawDogs broke up.

❖ The publishing office is now a
brokerage house.

❖ Borders went out of business.

—2010

Pieces of Mind

La Dolce Vita

A little boy in short pants jumping
in a puddle of freshly collected rain . . . a
bearded man with a blood-stained white
apron wrapped around his paunch
standing outside a butcher shop smoking
a cigarette, a boar's head hanging by a
string inside the window . . . a stunning
middle-aged woman wearing a short black
skirt, knee length leather boots, tight
jacket and slim eye-glasses, converses on
a phone while walking hurriedly past . . . a
young woman is black skirt, knee length
boots, tight jacket and thick, long, black
hair holds her boyfriend's hand while they
peer at the muddy Arno, which runs over
the banks this time of year . . . a squad of
uniformed Carabinieri drilling with
automatic rifles, trumpets and drums

while the tourists and smoking cafe patrons look curiously on . . .

These are just some of the sights and sounds I'm experiencing during my month long stay in Italy while I try and write the first draft the *Moonlight Rises* and while I complete *The Dead Souls*. It's also busy time because apart from seeing friends, I'm trying to tour the original trade paperback of my thriller, *The Remains*. We have something like 20 review commitments and every day brings a new challenge spreading the word. Same goes for *The Innocent*, the now bestselling re-release of *As Catch Can*. Both books have been big sellers out of the gate but I'm looking forward to these novels doing even better and reaching a bigger and bigger audience. Especially as the EBook and Kindle audience explodes over the Christmas Holiday. You fans should be able to collect my entire catalogue, including digital shorts for less than the price of a single Stephen King hardcover. Imagine that.

There's a woman yelling through the wall behind my bed. Someone is playing the flute. I hear a little boy singing and he's banging a drum. Tomorrow I will walk the streets of Florence in boots, jeans, and a leather jacket with the collar turned up. Some tourists will stop me and ask for directions. I will tell them that I am from New York. They will look puzzled. For a brief moment, we will be acting in the same Fellini film.

I will walk away.

Alone.

—2010

Pieces of Mind

Vincent Zandri: Sponsored by Budweiser Beer!

Lately there's been talk amongst publishers, agents, and authors alike that e-Books might one day be offered to the public for free (ok, I know this is happening now, but I mean ALL E-Books). Instead of the reader paying the author/publisher, sponsors will pay in exchange for product placement inside the text. Since the books are read via electronic reader, readers will be able to link to specific product websites, and even to that author's own books should the opportunity present itself.

I wondered if a scenario of sponsorship is realistic or if I even unintentionally mention the name of popular products and services inside the text of my books and more importantly, if I did so organically. In other words, do these products become included in the story because they belong there or because I might want them there in order to collect a payment?

Here's a small chapter of a new novel I'm working on, *Moonlight Rises* (the sequel to *Moonlight Falls*). Let's see how many instances of product placement there are without me forcing them into the text (I'm not gonna link to all of them because I'm a writer more than a blogger and I've got a lot of work to do . . . but you get the point!).

Darkness fills the bedroom.

How long had I been asleep? An hour? Three? It had to be at least three. I looked at my fifteen dollar Target special wrist watch. Fifteen past seven. I'd slept for over five hours. I slid off the bed, more than a bit groggy. There was some blood smeared on the bed sheet from where I rolled over onto my side. I touched my shirt and found that it was wet. I turned on the lamp, pulled off the shirt and the old dressing, checked the wound in the mirror above the dresser. The stitches were still intact. I put on a fresh dressing and a clean shirt. I'd slept long enough. Time to get to work. Find out if Paul Czeck was who he says he was, and if he was in fact looking for a man whom he swore he was his biological father.

I had the Dell laptop open on the kitchen counter, a Bud tall boy open beside it. Thank God for Verizon wireless internet. Allowed me to multi-task. I switched onto Google and typed in the name "Paul Czeck" in the search engine. Not a damn thing came up. Nothing about him belonging to a professional society of engineers, nothing regarding high school or college alumni. No

Facebook page, or Twitter account. As far as the internet and social media was concerned, Czeck was anonymous. And considering he worked for a facility that dealt on a daily basis with classified nuclear information, maybe that's the way it was supposed to be.

I sat back, took a sip of beer.

The pain in my side was getting worse. I tapped the wound gently with my fingers. It sent a small shockwave of sting up and down my side. The Lidocane had officially worn off. I got up, found the Advils in the cabinet above the sink, poured four into my hand. Sitting back down at the table, I swallowed all four with a swig of beer.

Next search. I got the website for The New York State Society for CPA's. Now there was some excitement. I typed in the name, Howard Roth. I got a single business address that was located downtown,

Broadway. Not far from where those three thugs beat the snot out of me. I wrote the address down on a Post-a-Note, stuffed it into my wallet. Tomorrow I'd go pay a visit to Mr. Roth's office, see if he did in fact look like the man in Czeck's black and white photo, only thirty-plus years older.

Next item. Maybe there was nothing noteworthy about Czeck on the web, but I could bet the mortgage he was located in the White Pages. And that's the way it turned out. He lived in a North Albany suburb called Loudonville. Four Orchard Grove. It's exactly where I would be heading that evening, soon as Georgie got here.

So there you have it. You count the instances of product placement. And I'll admit, I forced a couple in there, like the Target wrist watch one. But I did that to make a point: if as authors we wanted to cash in a on product placement, you see how easy it would be.

However, I was shocked to learn that popular products and services do appear more than I thought in my work. I wonder if they appear often enough for these companies to pay the author for their appearance much like film production companies collect a hefty payment for product placement in their popular movies? Only the future knows.

For now, I have to get back to work on the novel, and the all important climax which just happens to be taking place at *McDonalds* which this week is featuring oatmeal for breakfast and a return of the all beef, double . . .

—2011

The Business of Writing! The Art of Selling!

Back in 1922 a young writer who decided to move to Paris in order to pursue his muse was shocked to learn that many of the writers and artists who lived inside the famous city weren't really writers and artists at all. They were simply poseurs. Or posers.

People who sat about the cafes and pontificated upon the world of the arts, what was wrong with it, how they were going to somehow make a difference and turn everything that existed up until that moment onto its head. They would smoke and drink and drink and smoke, and talk and dress all in black and grow goatees and mustaches and they most certainly

looked like writers and artists, but in the
end they were a bunch of do nothing
nobodies. Yet it was these same poseurs
who came to hate the new eager young
writer. In him they recognized something
they lacked. He possessed drive. He
possessed energy. He possessed ambition.
And most of all, he possessed a talent that
would only come to fruition from both
hard work inside his writing studio and
hard work selling himself as an
adventurer and fearless sportsman to the
general public. He was the real deal and
for a long time, arguably "the most
interesting man in the world." That young
writer's name was Ernest Hemingway.

Just recently I attended a party
hosted by a quote—Artist—unquote. Many
artists were in attendance. Since I'm not
an entirely anonymous writer and thriller
author living in Albany, New York, I found
myself the brunt of some backhanded

jokes about my promotional "postings" for my recent bestsellers on the social networks. It was all supposed to be in good fun and I smiled and sucked it up. Ha Ha! The artists I'm referring to dress like artists. Long unwashed hair, chin beards, Salvation Army clothing. Some do yoga; some work in academia. One or two are extremely talented. A few others are talentless. They don't do gluten, and never, ever, do they utter a single non-PC word or phrase, unless of course, it's directed at someone not accepted inside their tight circle or someone they don't really like, such as a writer who not only spends his days writing but actively promoting his published work as though it were not an art necessarily, but a business.

But the truth is, writing is a business. Successfully selling your writing is an art.

My dad is going on 60 years in the commercial construction business. He is tremendously successful. He didn't get wealthy because he sat around talking about building. He didn't pretend to be a successful businessman by hanging around conferences, and country clubs, and ritzy bars buying expensive cocktails for pretty girls. He achieved success by working day and night, seven days a week. Often, he was scorned by other extended family members as being "all about his work." He was called "selfish" and "self-centered" by some of the very same people he put through school and later on, took care of financially. He wasn't so selfish then was he? I might not have followed in my dad's precise footsteps but I have learned an awful lot from him about running a business. His golden rule above all others? Work for yourself. Be your own boss, even if it means returning bottles and cans for the five cent refund for a while.

It's true, writing and the business of writing takes up a lot of time. Most of our time, that is if you are to pursue it to the best of your ability. And in my case, it can cost you dearly. I've been married twice and divorced twice. I still have difficulty maintaining a lasting relationship. I live in an apartment since I simply cannot keep up with a house. I travel often on assignment or out of pure wanderlust, because to sit in one place for too long is death for a writer. In a word, I am always working.

But the work is paying off in book sales that have quadrupled over the past year, and promise to quadruple again over the next six months. I am now lecturing to International Journalism students at the state university and in 2011 alone I will finish two new novels and write a good draft of another. I can't tell you how many articles, blogs, and digital shorts I will write but it will be a lot.

In the end, it's the work ethic that pays off. The follow-through, and finishing what you start. Just ask Ernest Hemingway. He is probably the best known of the Paris "Lost Generation." he is still a bestseller, nearly fifty years after his death. The poseurs who frequented the cafes and showed scorn for a "sell out" like Papa are long forgotten. They remain nobody. My dad, continues to run his business and works a 70 hours week at 75 years old. He is wealthy but he doesn't act like it. I also work every day, whether I'm traveling or not. In the new era of writers having to promote themselves through social media, blogs, virtual tours, appearances, book trailers, and more, there is no end to what has to be done. Plus you have to carve out precious time to write and read. Tough to maintain a family life at the same time, yet my kids aren't complaining. They too want to be writers.

Oh, and as for those artists I mentioned before . . . They need to work day jobs in order to support themselves. I don't have day job. A real one, that is. I work for myself. I'm a writer.

—2011

Pieces of Mind

Do You Miss Typewriters?

When I first got into this business, it was not uncommon to find writers who still used typewriters on a daily basis. Now, I'm talking 20 years ago. But it's a fact that back then, Jim Crumley, Robert Parker, Norman Mailer, Hunter Thompson, (hell, even Hemingway had he lived into his 80s) were using typewriters, even if they were powered electrically like the famous IBM Selectric.

'Course, all the writers I just mentioned are dead now, and so too it seems, is the typewriter.

I loved that famous picture of Papa seated at a desk in Ketchum, Idaho, looking healthy and burly, shirt sleeves rolled up to the elbows, while he pounded out the manuscript that would become *For Whom the Bell Tolls*. To me the sound of that machine-gun clatter only a typewriter can make is music to the soul. Especially the clatter from a manual typewriter. Back then I envisioned myself doing the same thing, typing out my stories and novels in single-extended-index-finger style on an old black Remington portable, not unlike the one Papa is using in the famous photo.

I'm a sucker for old typewriters and whenever I see one in an antique store or junk shop, I usually pick it up. I even wrote the first draft of *Moonlight Falls* on an old Olympic my wife Laura purchased for me at a garage sale way back when. I still have that typewriter, even though the ribbon is all used up. I do not however, have the wife.

I have another identical Olympic that is in pristine condition, ribbon and all. I also have an old Remington Rand Model No. 5 from the 30s or 40s, a pre-war Remington my grandfather used in Europe to type out his daily reports while fighting Germans in France and Germany. I have a one-hundred year old Remington that I can hardly lift (but it was probably considered the highly portable laptop of its day), and several other models, the names of which escape me now since I keep them down in a room set aside for me in my dad's office building.

Today I use a Dell Vostro 1320 Laptop, which I like a lot. I wrote *The Remains*, *Godchild*, and *The Innocent* on Dell laptops, after having penned them out in hand on blank yellow legal pads. In fact, I've gone through several laptops at this stage of the game, and at 46 and a half, I suspect I'll go through a lot more. I'm thinking maybe a MacAir 13" is in order since I travel so much.

I like laptops precisely because they remind me of the old typewriters, even though they don't have that romantic "ding" that happens every time the carriage reaches its limit, and you have to swing the carriage back in place with your right hand, locking and loading it for the next line. There's nothing like a good machine on which to make words and sentences. What I don't like about laptop computers is they grow slow, burn out, on occasion freeze up, or just shutdown altogether, and your work, some or all of it, is gone for good. Such are the risks of all mod cons.

I wonder, if Papa were alive today, what he would be writing on. Probably a laptop. I doubt he'd use a big desktop computer. They wouldn't be portable enough for a man who liked adventure almost as much as he did making up stories. I wonder how he'd feel about *For Whom the Bell Tolls* not only becoming an Amazon bestselling Kindle book, and at the same time, far outselling the paper versions.

Almost certainly he'd still be writing his manuscripts out by hand in blank note books (cahiers), several penknife-sharpened Ticonderoga No. 2's at the ready. Because even though typing and books have gone electronic and digital, one thing has not changed, nor will it ever change for a writer. And that's the enormous possibilities that exist, when you sit down at your writing desk in the early morning and do the existential stare-down with a blank page.

Vincent Zandri

—2011

Pieces of Mind

How We Write

There's a great scene in a movie called
HEMINGWAY (yah, with cap letters) that came
out about 20 years ago in which actor Stacey
Keach plays a rough, tough, marauding
Ernest Hemingway who says what he means,
means what he says and is willing to prove it
with his bare-knuckle fists.

The movie also portrays Papa
Hemingway sitting at a pool-side table in the
back yard of his Key West home, in front of
his typewriter, a bottle of whiskey handy by
his side. He's got the blood stained T-shirt on
from his fishing adventures on the Gulf
Stream, and he's pounding away at the keys of
the old Remington with muscular arms and a
tight but well fed belly. All around him people
are swimming and drinking and having fun.
His girlfriend is also present while his wife
occupies the house.

Nothing could be further from the truth.

Hemingway never wrote with a whiskey bottle on hand, nor did he make it a habit to write outside, preferring the solitude of his bedroom, but with the door open so that he could enjoy the muffled but somehow soothing ambient noise of the daily household routine. For the Nobel Prize winning author, writing fiction was not something you did when you drank. It was something to be approached with all the dedication and clarity of mind and memory of a monk. He often wrote standing up as often as possible, having once said of his craft and lifestyle, "Travel and writing can expand the mind, but also the ass." Hemingway was six feet tall.

That said, the late noir master, Jim Crumley once commented that he liked to drink beer when he wrote. When the writing was going well, he would actually burn off the alcohol as fast as he put it in. Crumley also liked to write standing up, but found it

difficult to find something that was the right
height. Crumley was five feet, ten inches.

Norman Mailer used to climb a rope
ladder that led the way up to a ship's mast
constructed inside his Brooklyn brownstone.
Once up the ladder he was forced to negotiate
a gangplank that led to his small loft studio.
One false move and down the Pulitzer Prize
winner would go, one full story. Mailer never
drank when he wrote preferring total sobriety,
and the occasional candy bar. He also never
wrote standing up. Mailer was five feet, eight
inches tall, but slightly less than four feet
sitting down.

I too try and write standing up, when I
can, but like Crumley, it's tough to find
something that's the right height. But like
Hemingway I use my bedroom (or hotel
rooms!), with the door slightly open so that I
can hear what's going on with the kids. I wrote
my first big novel *The Innocent* (*As Catch Can*)
to "Thomas the Train Engine" and Disney's
famous "Fantasia." I also wrote a full draft of
that novel up in an empty room inside an old

insurance agency that a friend offered up to me. I recall one morning he came into the room, coffee in hand and proceeded to tell me a joke about the three 'guinea pigs,' which was a kind of Mafioso take on the old Big Bad Wolf and the Three Pigs nursery rhyme. That joke immediately went into my novel, and gave it a kind of tongue and cheek boost that readers often comment on with a smile. Oh, and how tall am I? Five feet, seven and a quarter inches.

I don't drink when I write, but I have written dispatches from Europe for *RT* and other news agencies while having a drink or two at bar or cafe. Journalism doesn't distinguish between night and day so often times you have to drop everything to get a story out. That includes dropping a pretty good buzz or even a girlfriend if you have both going.

But as far as the fiction goes (and I'm at work on my 8th book now), I write clear-headed and sometimes with music going. I prefer the romantic tones of Ralph Vaughn Williams but lately have been listening to Phillip Glass. On occasion I'll play Zoot Simms and Bucky Pizzarelli for an added noir element. I try not to write with the internet engaged, nor do I pay attention to emails. Well, ok, sometimes I do. But I don't answer IMs. I could get an IM from the Virgin Mary when I'm writing and I would still ignore it.

I asked some FB peeps how they write and the answers I received were as varied as they were interesting. One person wrote with headphones on, the music "blaring" in her ears while she sometimes drinks coffee or tea, or even wine. Another gets up at 4 in the morning, thinks through the first cup of coffee, then hits the keys for the next one. Another insists on a broad view of her garden, and yet one more stressed the importance of exercise while engaged in a novel, having walked more than 40 miles per week during a recent novel draft.

This of course leads me back to Hemingway's, and my own, expanding ass.

I too can't stress enough the importance of exercise when writing. My second wife Laura would sometimes get upset that after having to be alone to write fiction all morning I would then insist on carving out a couple of hours to run a few miles and hit the gym for some weight training, or even boxing. Things would only get worse when, at the end of a writing day, I would want to head out to the corner joint for a couple of beers so that after a day of solitude, I might socialize a little and re-enter society.

No wonder writers make lousy husbands.

Today I'm writing sitting down. In a few minutes I'll go for a run, and then hit the gym. But I won't write this afternoon since I'm leaving for Europe tomorrow, and have some domestic chores to tend to. Like laundry for instance. But tomorrow morning, while I'm waiting for the first fight to board, I'll pull out the laptop, and write a story or maybe a new blog. I'm also bringing my new manuscript along, *Moonlight Rises*, so that I can keep on plowing through the latest draft. My publisher is expecting it very soon. In the next ten days I will write in Munich, Innsbruck, Venice, Florence, and Rome. I'll write in hotel rooms, bars, cafes, airports, train stations, trattorias. I'll write standing up and sitting down. I'll sometimes listen to music, and I'll drink espresso. Lots of espresso. Jet lag can be a real bitch especially when you're not fully recovered from the last bout of jet lag.

But I guess it really doesn't matter how or where I write, so long as I'm writing. Because in the words of author Jim Harrison, another writer who sometimes likes to write standing up, "your death, in those spooky terms, is stalking you every day."

Jim Harrison is five feet, nine inches.

—2011

Pieces of Mind

Venice "Carnival"

I haven't been to Venice in 23 years.

The first time I was there, I was 23.
That means I haven't been to Europe's most
famous, most romantic, most sinking, most
decaying, most don't-pinch-me-or-I'll-wake-up
paradise in a life time.

I wrote one of my most anthologized
and translated short stories not long after my
first visit to Venice. It was called, *Portrait*. It
was about getting lost but finding love within
the canals. Now, all these years later, with 5
novels behind me including *The Remains* and
Godchild, I'm finding that Venice, although a
maze, isn't nearly as confusing or intimidating
as it was all those years ago. I guess maturity
has its advantages. So does grace under
pressure.

This is the time of Carnival and it
seems as though the entirety of Italy has

descended upon the ancient city. People of all
ages, wearing costumes and gowns and masks
make for a mysterious if not dangerous
experience. Even if it is all in good fun.
Tossed into the sea of people are women in
ball gowns topped with white wigs, faces
painted with white powder. Men wear black,
shin-length, capes, and those triangular caps
that the great lover Casanova wore. Some
wear evil masks of grossly long noses, while
other people . . . young, college age, silly
people . . . dress up in bunny costumes.
The point, as I understand it, is first, to be
photographed by the hordes of journalists and
photographers who've come to record the
event for their various publications. But also
the point is to celebrate the dead and the
coming Lenten season, which I assume is why
the final day of Carnival takes place at
precisely the same time Fat Tuesday happens
in New Orleans.

Or I could be of course wrong about all
this.

But I do know this, the masks and costumes were originally meant to disguise one's self from one's class, which means, even back in the olden days, Venetians of all shapes, sizes and bank accounts were looking to get it on with one another.
Why do I say that?

Because like all good festivals, Carnival ain't just about the funny costumes. It's a lot about the booze and what happens *after* the booze.
Case and point?

The groans and moans of ecstasy coming from the young Japanese couple in the room directly beside my own. Makes me feel kind of left out.
Back to all those people . . .

It's hard during this festival to find alone time.

There are so many people on this fish shaped island (30,000 pour in per day!), it's not hard to imagine it sinking once and for all. But you can still find some peace and quiet away from the tourist areas like San Marco.

So much peace and quiet and business as usual exists in the "ghetto," or what was once the Jewish District, that this morning, I was able to jog up and down a cobblestone jetty without once running into a single soul.

Man or woman.

Being thrust into a pool of masked humanity has its frustrations if not downright scary moments, such as patting your back pocket for your wallet and not feeling the usual hard bulge, but only then, forgetting you slipped it into the interior pocket of your leather jacket. For safe keeping.

. . . *Wipes sweat from his brow with the back of his hand* . . .

But there are gifts here that are uniquely Venice.

There's the gondola ride on the Grand Canal and over the feeder canals, the gondolier singing softly while pushing the sleek black boat over narrow canals made of decaying brick, filled up with green, thick looking water. There's the pastry shops that smell of fresh baked cakes and sweets and bread, and how good the cafe tastes with a raspberry filled croissant still warm from the oven. There's the antique shops, and jewelry shops, and wine shops that sell bottles for only 5 Euros. And of course, there's exhausted waiters who give you a grumpy look and even grumpier service when serving a masterpiece of shrimps cooked in hot spices over a bed of fresh polenta.

Venice has been sinking for years, or so they say. But my gut tells me that I will be sunk far earlier than this ancient city on the sea. If I keep coming here every 23 years, I will be 69 during my next visit. Assuming I live one more block of 23 years beyond that, I will be 92, that is I'm doing my math right.

I'm imagining myself at 92.

Old, crooked, slow, and maybe sad. But Venice will be the same. And even though I will be passing on, I will walk the same cobbles I once walked as a young man, as many young men did before me. And it will be like living a memory.

Past, present and future.

Pieces of Mind

—2011

Vincent Zandri

Why I Still Publish Traditionally

No I don't live under a rock.

I'm well aware that the "in thing" these days is to self-publish. Jeeze, remember the golden olden days (like 6 months ago . . .), when an author who even muttered the words "self-published" was considered the worst kind of vain vermin, especially to MFA in Writing School types and college poetry professors?

Well, the world has changed and more than one self-published author, Amanda Hocking among them, have gone from absolute nobodies to multi-millionaires within a period of about a year. Having sold more than a million of her paranormal thrillers on Kindle and E-Book, Amanda just signed a deal worth two mill at St. Martin's Press. Big news in New York City, not to mention a watershed event of Tsunami proportions.

But wait a minute . . . hold the phone. Didn't I just point out that the cool thing to do these days is to self-publish? And why would a writer who is already making a million bucks decide to upset the "program" if you will, and make the switch to a traditional major publisher?

In a word: TIME.

Upon accepting her new deal, Ms. Hocking expressed a desire to spend her day "writing" and not formatting HTML and designing covers. Self-publishing might place all the control and money into the author's pocket, but it's a mammoth time sucker.

Which brings me to my original point. Why do I still publish traditionally when I could double my royalties by going DIY?

TIME.

I'm both a journalist and a fiction writer. I write and edit more than 36 small pieces per month, plus write three "professional" blogs (these blogs are more like full-length articles), and in addition, maintain my own growing blog. And, at present, I have three books going plus I'm expecting a galley proof for my forthcoming new novel *The Concrete Pearl*. On top of this, I have to begin roughing out what will be the sequel to "*Pearl*." Plus I have kids, I travel a lot, and I like to work out, eat, and drink . . . In other words, I want to have a life, not a *live-in-significant-other* relationship with my freakin' computer.

Therefore I have an agent (or in my case agents . . .), and I have a publisher (or three) who edit, publish, and distribute my books for me, and in exchange they take percentage of each sale, because they deserve it.

Like I already said, I ain't living under a rock these days, and any publisher, from small indie to the biggest major, which is faring well in the marketplace knows that the book producing paradigm has changed significantly. Publishers are no longer Gods living high up on "You can't get there from here mountain!" They've become humbled as of late, and therefore, their attitudes on the working relationship with the author has shifted from Land Owner/Indentured Servant to Partner/Partner.

Nowadays an author provides the publisher with great work, and the publisher provides the author with great and necessary services. Traditional publishers will:

- ❖ Take your book on only if it's an exceptional read (Yes, this is a service believe it or not. Self-pub'd authors run the risk of unleashing absolute crap on the reading public!)
- ❖ They edit and proof your work.
- ❖ They take the time to provide your opus with the best, most eye catching cover possible (remember, in these the days of E-Books you can judge a book by its cover)
- ❖ They package, distribute, and market your book.

* They do your accounting, collect your money, and send you a check.
* If your book isn't selling well, they will assist you in improving those sales.

Of course, publishers do more than this, but even those few services mentioned above are enough to keep me publishing traditionally.

I remember taking flying lessons right when I got out of college. After about my fifth or sixth lesson, the flight instructor pulled me aside and suggested that I remain a passenger rather than become a pilot. In his opinion, I just didn't quite have the organizational skills it takes to become a pilot who maintains a life rather than crashing and burning. Somehow I get the feeling that if I were to attempt self-publishing, I'd forget a few of the necessary steps and, well, crash and burn.

I don't regret my decision.

With the assistance of my publishers, I am currently selling 1,000 copies of *The*

Innocent per day, and if it keeps moving the way it has been, it will become the Number 1 bestselling Amazon Kindle Book in the world (it's No. 29 as of this writing; No. 2 in Hard-Boiled Mysteries). The sequel, *Godchild*, is close on its tail, and *The Remains* is close on its tail . . .

So one more time . . . Why do I still publish traditionally?

TIME!

And For bestselling Kindle author Vincent Zandri, there is simply no other way.

—2011

Responsible Publishing, Big Breakout Success!

A lot of my peeps have been chiming in asking me what it feels like to be selling a whole bunch of Kindle E-Books these days on Amazon. Like thousands, per day. No kidding. That ain't no typo. Not bad numbers for a former construction worker. Go figure! (Me, shaking my head in disbelief, but also looking up to the heavens with gratitude!)

But the truth is, I'm not entirely sure how to feel about it. Currently I'm the number 4 overall bestselling Kindle and have been as high as number 3. Two of the three authors above me are propped up by major motion pictures (Hope I get a move produced one day!). Since the middle of March I have moved around 31,000 units of *The Innocent,* and *Godchild* it's sequel, is about to enter into the Top 100 books also.

But back to how I feel about it.

I feel great, naturally. Who wouldn't feel great? It's cool to be popular. I thought there might be some talk about the pricing, but the sale price of a buck is only temporary and my other books, like *The Remains*, that are priced at the normal $2.99 are selling in the low hundreds. Even the $9.00 *Moonlight Falls* has gained something like 200% in the rankings and is holding steady, if not slowly gaining more ground, which tells me a lot of my fans are willing to pay an extra few dollars for my brand of "quality" thriller and mystery (Thank you!!!).

So, the question still persists: How do I feel?

First of all, I am honored that I am earning ("earning" being the keyword here) a fan base that is willing to support my work, and enjoy it. I owe you not only a lot, but I owe you everything. And in return I will keep putting out very good books. I will write to the best of my ability every day. But second of all, I am being cautious. Cautious because I've been to the show once before with the majors and realized that success in this business can be volatile to say the least.

However, my success now is notably different than before.

My association and "success" with the big guys in New York was initially measured by one thing and one thing only: The size of the advance. Back in '99 I received a quarter of a million dollar advance for two books. And after the pub experienced an internal shakeup, my books along with a whole bunch of others, were simply tossed to the side. The end result was that I couldn't even begin to earn back my advance. Add to that, the big chain bookstores pulling the paper off the shelves after six weeks, and you smell a recipe for disaster.

Success this very minute is far different.

By that, I mean I am now being published responsibly.

What does responsible publishing entail?

The author earns what he or she sells. It's as simple as that, and it is not a new idea by any stretch of the imagination. Back when Hemingway started, authors might receive a very tiny advance, but they were paid by how many books they sold. Book runs were small, and essentially POD. The evil system of returns had not yet been conceived of by the booksellers association. Authors didn't have agents, and they weren't issued a pile of money they couldn't begin to pay back. Not without their book becoming a No. 1 bestseller and staying there for ten weeks. In a word, the system worked.

Responsible publishing not only means earning what you sell, but it means building an audience and pleasing that audience as best you can. Which means offering them sales like books for a buck, or doubles for five bucks, and making sure you earn every penny of that currency with great writing and a cool cover. Every penny that's earned is yours and your publisher's to keep. If you self-publish, you get the whole pot after you pay off your subcontracted editors, artists, etc.

I feel that my numbers will probably level off at some point, but will stay in low hundreds territory for a long, long time. Other indie authors are proving that the new responsible publishing model tends to work this way. Authors like Joe Konrath, LJ Sellers, Debbie Mack and so many others are doing what a whole lot of big advance authors working out of New York are not doing: They are selling in droves. And what's more, we're talking E-Books here. These books are not coming off the cyber shelves anytime soon or at all for that matter. Maybe *The Innocent* is No. 3 or 4 overall today, and given time and price changes, may slide down to 50 or even 200. But with some revised package enhancement and new pricing, that same book could be the no. 1 overall bestseller two years from now when my audience might be four or five times as large. The book will once again be re-introduced to a whole new group of readers from around the globe.

So again, how do I feel about having a breakout bestseller or two?

Like the old Beatles song goes, I feel fine.

But I'm also guarded and I'm not about to quit my journalism entirely. I'm not about to diminish my marketing efforts. I will however be cutting back on certain trade journalism projects in order to write more fiction. Because like newbie indie and bestselling author Barry Eisler recently pointed out, the best way for an author to maximize his or her sales earning potential is by writing more books.

Which is why I'm going to end this blog and get back to the fiction.

—2011

Back to the Old School

I was the guest speaker at my old high school yesterday afternoon as a part of their quote, "Distinguished Alumni," unquote program. It's a little hard to swallow being referred to as a distinguished anything in Vin World, considering I put my socks on one at a time just like everyone else, the only difference being my socks probably have holes in them and maybe I've been wearing them for a couple of days now. I'm a bachelor. You gotta let me slide on certain things, like clean clothes for instance.

Ok, back to school.

A little background. My old school, The Albany Academy, was once a private, all boys, military academy. It's also old. Really old, having been established in 1813. When I attended the place from 1978-1982, the military component was still in full swing. We wore uniforms that matched West Point's, and drilled on a daily basis. The halls of our bottom floor were lined not with posters of peace, love, and understanding, but Springfield 03-A3 rifles. We had a shooting range upstairs, a Major, a Colonel, and strict haircut regulations. Anyone who received a certain amount of demerits at inspection was expected to march around the front "flag-pole" circle, even if it was raining.

It was all good fun . . . *Wink.*

Some pretty big notables, literary and otherwise, have passed through the Academy's corridors through the years including, Herman Melville, the Roosevelt kids, and even Andy Rooney.

The school has changed radically since my time. It has now merged with the girl's school located across the street. Participation in the military is no longer required, but instead a "volunteer" extracurricular activity. The West Point uniforms are gone, giving over to preppy blue blazers, rep-ties, and khakis. Gone are the guns, the Colonel's, the inspections, and, in a word, the junk that used to keep me up at night.

The place has evolved into a country day prep school that boasts a whole bunch of happy-go-lucky students, and that to me is a refreshing sight to see (Believe me, when I was there I used to sweat out the polish on my shoes, not to mention my math homework, and holy crap, Herman Melville went here. When do we start reading Moby Dick?).

I was greeted by the new headmaster, who immediately took my hand in his, and told me he was reading *The Remains* on Kindle, and that he was "loving it." This same man graduated from the school in 1958 and despite our generation gap, proudly pronounced his love of the E-Book. When I told him how many I was selling these days (2-3,000 per day) he nearly fell over. Next on his list is *The Innocent*. I promised him a nice endowment if my sales keep up . . . *Wink again*

Then came the moment of absolute truth.

187

Pieces of Mind

I was led to a podium inside the "Chapel" where I began to deliver an address to two-hundred or so students and faculty. I spoke about writing my first story at the school, and the influence one writing teacher by the name of Frank Nash had on me. Nash had turned me onto Papa Hemingway and from that day forward I knew I wanted to be like the adventurous writer. I wanted to do what he did, minus the suicide of course.

I offered bulleted advice to the students regarding the writing life, which included, "Live in Europe for a year," "Don't get married," and "You must learn to develop the ability to write interestingly about a teabag," a quote which originates from my *RT* South African journalist colleague, Lizette Potgeiter. By the time I was finished with my worldly advice the students were applauding, laughing, cheering. And then something strange happened.

From what I was told later, the students almost never raise their hands and pose questions at the completion of a

Distinguished Alumni speech. Being kids, they usually want to get the hell out to burn some steam. But in this case, dozens of hands were raised while some pretty intelligent questions were posed to me. Everything from, "Do you speak Italian?" (not yet) to "What are your books about (check out my website www.vincentzandri.com), to "Are you Harrison Zandri's father?" (Yup, he's home writing his first novel and bench pressing 250 pounds).

I'll be honest here. It isn't easy going back to your old school. I was a crappy student, and usually ended up in summer school for math. Some of my classmates must surely be more distinguished than I am. Andy Rooney graduated from the school for God's sakes. I couldn't imagine what I had accomplished that would make the school want me to share my wisdom with the students. With these thoughts stirring in the back of my brain, I simply spoke the truth.

But later on, when it was all over, the headmaster once more warmly shook my hand, and he told me something that will stick with me forever. He told me that the advice I offered the kids was "real." And that's why they invited me back to school, and *keeping it real* is what made the difference in their young lives, if only for one brief sun-filled afternoon in April.

—2011

New York Times . . . Helllllooooooo?????

I'm selling more books than Stephen King right now.

Ok . . . E-Books.

Kindle E-Books to be even more specific.

And I have been for about a month now since *The Innocent* broke the Amazon Kindle TOP 100 and settled into the TOP 10 where it's been holding under the No. 5 spot for more than two weeks.

You with me here????

Believe me when I tell you, I am super proud of this accomplishment. So is my publisher. But here's where it gets a little sticky for me. When I look at The New York Times Bestseller list for "E-Books," it lists the first two bestsellers, *The Lincoln Lawyer*, followed by *Water for Elephants*, but then it skips me and lists *The Land of Painted Caves* as next in line . . . far as I can tell, "*Painted Caves*" doesn't appear anywhere on the Amazon Top Ten.

What am I missing here?

The Innocent has sold almost 50,000 copies in the past FOUR weeks alone. It's currently moving around 2,000 to upwards of 3,000 units per day. My novels *Godchild* and *The Remains* follow close in its wake. All combined (and I'm not even including the ten to fifteen copies per day *Moonlight Falls* sells at $8.99), I'm looking at around 3,000 to 3,500 Kindle units moved per day. Yet the NYT doesn't acknowledge it.

Could it be that my Barnes and Nobles sales, although good, haven't quite caught up to the Amazon sales?

Could it be that *The Innocent* was published previously under a Random House imprint?

Could it be that I'm a traditionally pub'd indie?

Should my agent be getting on the horn?

I don't have the answers. But I've seen evidence where even self-pub'd authors will on occasion be included in the list. Like Amanda Hocking or Debbie Mack. But maybe their inclusion is not the norm. Because if the NYT were to include more self-pub'd and indie authors, I believe they would dominate the list. LJ Sellers would be there. Joe Konrath would be there. So would CJ West, and so on, and so forth.

Ok, I couldn't be happier about this past month, and I could not be more thankful. But I'm just curious as to how the NYT decides what to include in their list and what not to include, and well, if it even matters anymore.

However, how cool would it be to tell my parents I made the NYT list or USA Today?

My guess is that if I hang in there, and keep writing good books, it will happen. But by then, I might not really care all that much about it . . . Ah, who you kiddn' Zandri, yes you will!!!

—*2011*

Vincent Zandri

How I Sold 100,000 EBooks in 60 Days:
A Letter to my Mom

Dear Mom,

For the one-thousandth time, NO, I'M NOT GOING TO GET A 'REAL JOB!' I don't need to. I just sold over 100,000 E-Books in 60 days. Yah, that's right mom. That's not a typo. No I'm not drunk again, and no I'm not smoking crack or puffing on whacky weed. I don't do drugs.

But I sold 100,000 books and I did it with the help of my new publisher. Ok, I know, I've had publishers before. Big publishers who gave me a quarter-million bucks in advance for a couple of books that barely made it off the runway before crashing and burning. I know the embarrassment it

195

caused you at the beauty parlor while all those chatty women kept asking you, "Whatever happened to your son? Does he still write?" Well, now you can tell them I hit the 100,000 book club, and when they look at you with disbelieving eyes from under the bulbous transparent hair-dryers and ask you how on earth I did it, you can tell them this:

1. I'm obsessed with my numbers. Kindle numbers. So what's the first thing I do in the morning even before getting out of bed, I check my numbers via my Blackberry. The information grounds me and gives me a sense of which book or books I might want push that day.

2. Then, after making the coffee and washing up, I hit the Facebook. While in the old days I might have posted something stupid like, "Buy my new book *THE INNOCENT*!" I rarely go for that direct marketing approach anymore. Better to take the indirect approach. My FB friends get kind of sick of me asking them to always buy, buy, buy. Better to

simply post your thoughts and feelings for that moment in time. Even if they're just silly. People can relate to "I could go for a beer right now!" better than they do, "Buy This Book!" It's the difference between becoming a real person someone likes and enjoys as a friend, as opposed to a used car salesman whom they most definitely do not. And if people like and appreciate you for who you are, they will probably give your books a try. I.E. Ernest Hemingway and Norman Mailer didn't survive as bestsellers on talent alone: they spent a great deal of time building their cult of personality.

3. While still on Facebook, I might check out some of the pages I belong to like Amazon Kindle and NOOK. While once a week, I'm allowed to push one of my books like directly on the pages, I use these forums more to contribute to whatever conversation is at present going on. Or if there isn't a particular thread being explored, I might start one, such as "Are Mommy Bloggers More Powerful than

the New York Times Review of Books?" E-Book readers are a chatty bunch and they don't consider their electronic reading devices simply a means for reading the latest and greatest. That e-reader gripped in their hands means they belong to an exclusive club. That club allows its many voices to be heard on the FB pages. It's fun for readers and fans to hear from the authors they are reading now and again.

4. Same goes for KindleBoards. After hitting up the FB pages, I might log onto that site and either contribute to an ongoing topic at the Writer's Cafe, or post my own topic. Being on KindleBoards lets other authors like me know that I care enough about their triumphs and pitfalls to comment on them. We offer encouragement when things are bad, and kudos when things are going well. It's sort of like a student union for writers.

5. From there I navigate my way to my other online communities . . . My Twitter, my

Edgy Christian Fiction, my Goodreads, my Crimespace, my LinkedIn, and more. if I don't have something to post there in their respective blog sections, I'll maybe provide a real-time status update, such as, 'I'll be appearing on Suspense Magazine's Blog Talk Radio . . . ' I'll offer up a link to the program along with the time and date of my scheduled appearance.

6. Once all that's done, I might take an hour to write a new blog for *The Vincent Zandri Vox*. The blog topic will usually be one that has to do with writing or publishing. On occasion, I'll write about my experiences in marketing my work. Other writers, especially newbies are starving for information and stories from those who have been there before them. Especially from authors who have been published by both the Big 6 and the Indies like myself. They like to get the inside scoop on what it's like to be more or less screwed over by a company like Random House only to emerge from the dark wilderness and into the

welcome arms of an indie publisher. Many of these new authors are also interested in the self-publishing process. But that's more for a very popular blog like JA Konrath's, "A Newbies Guide to Publishing" blog. I highly recommend it for the DIY author.

7. When the blog is completed, it's time to make it viral (no mom, I'm not trying to make people sick!). That means I'll post it to all the social networks like FB, Twitter, Delicious, Google Buzz, Myspace, Digg . . . you name it. If the blog is discussion worthy, I'll re-post it to KindleBoards and a few other discussion-related groups and forums I belong to on FB, Yahoo, Crimespace, and even Goodreads. Lastly, I'll post the new blog on my fan page and my FB page for *The Vincent Zandri Vox.*

8. If I have a virtual tour going on, I'll want to check in on the tour-stop of the day, which can be a review, a guest blog post, an interview, or even a live chat which usually

will happen in the evening after dinner. On occasion I might have a blog talk radio scheduled for that day, which can run about an hour.

9. At some point in the day, I'll want to email some fellow authors and ask them for guest posts for *The Vincent Zandri Vox*, because your author blog shouldn't be narrow or static. It shouldn't be all about you! It should be a communal place where not only my books and opinions are discussed, but a whole range of books and topics.

10. At some point in the day, I'll check in with my publisher. We'll strategize and make plans over which books we have coming out when, such as the new special edition combo I have going with the great noir legend, Dave Zeltserman (*Dying Memories*/*Godchild*) and my brand new forthcoming novel, *Concrete Pearl*. Or we'll talk pricing. The great thing about being with an indie publisher is that they have a lot of freedom to experiment

with pricing. My publisher understands the importance of offering up a great book for the lowest price possible. Wow, what concept, huh mom? Our pricing strategy for now is based on the concept of the "rotation." An author should always have one or two books available at $.99 and maybe another couple at $2.99, perhaps one at $4.99 and, as is the case with my catalog, even one at $8.95. Having some books on sale ensures that your audience is always expanding and even though you might invite a bad review or two by underpricing your books temporarily, the benefits inherent with creating new fans far outweigh the negatives. In any case, all this pricing stuff is a work in progress.

11. Ok, so when all that's done, it's time to think about the real thing behind the success. The writing. What's the most surefire way to sell 100,000 e-books in 60 days? Good, if not great writing. And great writing takes time. It can't be rushed, even if this is the new era of authors meeting the challenge of

publishing two, three, and in some cases, four books per year—a feat unheard of back when I was publishing with the biggies. E-books are forever, and never will they go out of print. So, for as long as a book still resides in your gray matter and not on the printed cyber-page (and yes, mom, trade paperback!), it's not earning money. However, putting lots of books out for public consumption doesn't mean skimping on quality. What's the fastest way to guarantee never to sell 100,000 e-books in 60 days again? Bad writing.

Well, I hope this gives you some idea of what it takes to sell all those books, mom. And I guess you can see now how impossible it would be for me to have a real job. I work seven days a week right now as it is. Talk about a time consuming career. Don't believe me? Just ask your two ex-daughter in-laws. I'm sure they'd both have something to say on the topic.

But let me ask you something else, mom.

What real job out there would pay me close to $20,000 in a single month to do something I absolutely love? Would I get 20 Gs per month project managing construction projects? Would I get 20Gs per month if I were an accountant? Would I get 20 G's per month if I were teaching high school? If I were writing public relations and advertising copy?

Probably not, which is why I choose to be a full-time writer in this, the new golden age of publishing.

I have to go now, mom. Lots of work to do. Tell dad, I said hi! And I hope you guys can come and visit me in Italy soon. Oh, yeah, did I forget to tell you that I can write and conduct my writing business from anywhere in the world???? Now try and do that with a real job and two weeks vacation per year!

All my love,
Vince
—2011

Pieces of Mind

"One True Sentence"

Then there was a young man who no
longer wanted to pursue a traditional
education. That young man would be my son,
Harrison, whom we refer to as "Bear" because
he looks like one in every bit of that cuddly,
dark, and furry curl-up-to-him kind of way.
Recently the Bear came to me to ask if he
could stop attending his high school (where he
was an A student) in order to pursue a writing
career. Naturally I was both thrilled and
frightened by this notion. While on one hand I
was happy that he wanted to engage in a
career that has become my own life-passion, I
was also concerned that he too would have to
experience many of the pitfalls, calamities,
frustrations, depressions, losses too many to
count, and all those hardships that can go
with the writing life, not to mention being
scary broke at times.

But having expressed my feelings to him (and some of these so called "expressions" occurred in the form of heated discussions to say the least), I acquiesced to his desires. And I did so for one reason and one reason only. I wanted him to be happy.

Fast forward to the present.

That said, the young literary neophyte hasn't given up his education. It's just that his education is no longer the traditional public high school You-Read-What-We-Tell-You-To-Read-Or-Else program. Now, I'm more or less home-schooling the Bear and in the process, utilizing my library of paper books and his brand new Kindle as a learning tool.

We've been focusing a lot on Hemingway as a foundation, since Papa was so instrumental in my own education and also because the public high schools of today have fallen out of favor with Hemingway as not being "PC." This past Sunday we sat down for two hours to watch a two-part biography on Ernest Hemingway produced by the BBC in the mid-1980s that I had video-taped off the television back when I wasn't that much older than the Bear. Having watched the program for the first time in years, I was once again struck by Hemingway's notion of wanting to write "one true sentence;" how as a young writer struggling to write his first publishable stories in 1920's Paris, Hemingway came up with the idea that if he could only write the truest sentence he knew, then the rest of the words would follow. When the writing was finally going well, he could stop for the day in a place where he would know what would happen next. That way he could be assured of continuing on the next day with, of course, another "true sentence."

Writing from a cold room that overlooked a sawmill in the Montparnasse section of Paris, Hemingway expressed the difficulty in trying to write one true sentence along with the story that would follow. On the days "it wouldn't come," he would have to remind himself that he had written before and he would most definitely write again. But in his words, you not only sense an overriding fear or anxiety that it might never come again, you also sense a tragic prophecy in the making:

"Do not worry. You have always written before and you will write now. All you have to do is write one true sentence. Write the truest sentence that you know."

I remember a writing teacher of mine giving a lecture to the student body of my MFA school up in Vermont posing the question: "What the hell does 'one true sentence mean?'" I guess in the usual academic sense of beginning with a subject and adding a verb to it in order to spark some action and inevitably a plot, the concept of "one true sentence" might not exactly fit the bill for would-be writers trying to learn their chops. But in the context of where Hemingway was at in his young life, and how his entire well-being would come to depend upon that first sentence, and the one that would follow that, and the one that would follow that, "true" begins to take on another meaning entirely other than something that is real, or that had certainly happened, or that he had personally witnessed. True begins to take on a more philosophical context of self. Rather, in this case, the existential parts (or personalities) that make up the self and that are constantly at battle with one another.

In learning to write one true sentence, Hemingway was chiseling away the rock that was his outer shell, and revealing his true being. He was striving to reveal his inner core and the hell of it is, is that he had no choice but to engaged in the impossible task all alone. The young man who would come to write unmistakably stylized classic like *Big Two-Hearted River*, *A Farewell to Arms*, *For Whom the Bell Tolls*, and *The Old Man and the Sea*, would reflect this battle with the individual self in his anti-hero characters who will have no choice but to fight and die alone, and do so "tragically." This individual battle with the self to write one true sentence is precisely the process my son is just starting to go through, and that I still go through every day when I place a pencil to a blank sheet of paper or face the infinite blankness of the computer screen. This sense of not knowing what will happen, and having no one to depend upon other than yourself to make it happen. That's what it means to write one true sentence, and it doesn't surprise me in the least that an MFA in Writing Prof would miss the point entirely.

It's a frightening reality contemplating the day when that one true sentence won't come anymore. For Bear, that doesn't seem to be a possibility while he spends his days learning his craft and mortality to him is at best a vague concept. It doesn't for me either, as I enter into my middle years and hopefully, my stride as a prolific author and journalist. What I worry about more are the later years, when our faculties fail us as human beings, and the writing, which takes as much emotional, mental, and physical strength as it does creativity, doesn't come as easily. That time when we face the void and the void wins out.

In the early summer of 1961, Hemingway the man of blood, bone and flesh, was beginning to fail. And it took a toll on his ability to write his "one true sentence." In his own words spoken with tear-filled eyes to his then private doctor, George Saviors, MD, Papa sadly admitted, "It just won't come anymore, George."

That's when Hemingway performed the last, most truest final act of his life by placing both barrels of a shotgun inside his mouth, pressing them up against the soft upper palate, and thumbing back the triggers.

—2011

Pieces of Mind

Write What You Know (A Father's Day Essay!)

What's the first thing you learn in Creative Writing 101?

"Write what you know!"

For young authors who haven't yet experienced a whole lot of life, that can be a rather daunting idea. but for those of us who have been around the block a few times, there's always a story or two we can write about, such as the night I spent alone in a Sing Sing prison cell, or the time I was stranded in the jungle in Benin, Africa, after our 4X4 bit got stuck in a swamp.

But then, sometimes you don't have to look too far in order to tap into a life experience. Sometimes you just have to take another look at the way you were raised. In my case, I was raised in a family of construction workers. And by the time I reached puberty, my dad's business had taken off to a level where he went to work in pressed trousers and button-down oxford instead of jeans and work boots. In fact, my dad's business began doing so well, he groomed me for taking over the business one day.

Truth be told, the grooming began very early on. I helped my dad lay out a new church he was contracted to build at age 5. I still recall holding the tape measure for him while he recorded the measurements in his notebook. At around age 12 I was in charge of recording telephone quotations should he be bidding a big job during my summer vacations. At 15 I worked on my first job-site and stepped on a sixpenny nail that impaled itself through my foot. At 20 I was assigned to the office where I read blueprints and helped expedite projects. By 23 I was managing construction jobs worth $6 million or more. That's when I quit to become a full-time writer.

My dad was heartbroken, but not disappointed. After all a dad only wants his kid to be happy, right? And he was happy for me that I'd found something to be as passionate about as he was his business. All he worried about was my being able to make a living, so when books like *THE INNOCENT* and *THE REMAINS* became bestsellers, he jumped for sheer joy higher than I did.

But all is not lost on my having essentially experienced an entire career in the commercial construction business. I put it to use in my new thriller, *CONCRETE PEARL*, starring brassy but bold construction business owner, Ava "Spike" Harrison. How did she get the nickname Spike?

Well she stepped on a sixpenny nail of course, first day out on a real construction job-site. When it comes to writing what you know, the apple should not fall far.

But I appreciate all that my dad did for me when I was growing up and trying to find my way, the least of which is giving me a real insiders look at a world of builders, designers and architects that remains fascinating to me, even if I no longer carry a hammer or work on blueprints. Oh, and as for Spike, she's not only a builder, she's an amateur woman sleuth who carries a framing hammer as an equalizer instead of a gun . . . you might want to kiss her, but you sure as hell don't want to mess with her.

Happy Father's day, Dad! Oh, and thanks!!!

—*2011*

So What Are You: Indy or Anal?

If I had a nickel for every time I got asked the question, "Are you a seat-of-the-pants kind of writer or a planner?" In other words, am I bull who just barrels ahead without mapping out my scenes ahead of time in the hopes of allowing my story to form naturally or what all the no-gluten-professor geeks at writing school call, "organically?" Or do you actually write up character sketches that include everything from place of birth to bathroom habits, and then map out each chapter detail for detail?

The answer I give is not really an answer.

"It depends on the book," I tell them. "And it also depends on the character."

If I'm writing a book like *THE REMAINS* that's intended to be stand-alone literary thriller that contains subject matter such as identical twins, modern art and autistic savants and that is also told from the P.O.V. of a women, you can bet your bottom ten-spot that I'm gonna plan it out ahead of time. I'm also going to do some meticulous research so that those Brown Shirt sabotage reviewers on Amazon don't try and crucify me yet again (Screw 'em!). In the end if I've done my job right and the writing is convincing enough, I just might have a bestseller on my hands. And *THE REMAINS* has been just that. A bestseller for over a year (And many thanks to those who have reviewed responsibly and spent precious time writing mature and critically appreciated reviews. I love you!)

But if I'm writing a novel like one of the Dick Moonlight Serials, now that's another story altogether. The Richard "Dick" Moonlight of *MOONLIGHT FALLS*, *MOONLIGHT MAFIA*, and the forthcoming *MOONLIGHT RISES* and *MURDER BY MOONLIGHT* is a total train wreck of a guy. He's got a little piece of .22 caliber bullet lodged inside his brain from a failed suicide attempt. The piece has lodged itself right beside his cerebral cortex causing him the occasional short term memory lapse and lack of judgement, especially under times of stress, which is usually always. He drinks too much, and he can also pass out at any time or even suffer stroke, coma and death. In a word, Moonlight has no clue if he'll be alive from one minute to the next. So his relentless search for right over wrong is always an unplanned adventure. Since he narrates all of his own stories, I feel the best way to write his books is to do so by the seat-of-my-pants. And thus far anyway, you loyal readers of mine (you know who you are), have sort of fallen in love with the dude. And that's a cool thing since he's the character who is most like me.

So what's the best way for you to write your book?

Remember when you'd ask you mom or dad what was for dinner, and not having decided on anything yet, they might ask you in return, "Well what do you feel like?" A lot of what we decide to put in our body is based not only on a craving but more so on what our bodies are lacking at that time. If we're protein starved we want meat or chicken. If were worn out and carb poor, we want pasta or even pizza.

It's the same with writing. Listen to your body and your brain, but most of all listen to your gut. Not your gut mind you, but the gut inside your main character. Is he or she someone who will want to be guided and reigned in? Or is he or she someone who won't plan for the next five minutes much less two afternoons from now?

Just remember, writing is a personal venture and there is no right or wrong way to do it. There is only just doing it.

—2011

Pieces of Mind

Vincent Zandri

The Meaning of Life

Life is all about change.

That's no secret.

We should be changing every day if we are to grow as human beings. We don't need constant radical change, because that's not cool. There's got to be some semblance of stability in the life if we are to be healthy enough to experience positive change. See how that works?

But there are times in our lives when radical change does occur through no fault of anyone or anything other than time catches up. In my case, my oldest son, Jack, is about to turn 21 in late October, and my lease on the apartment I've had now in North Albany for six years will expire on the same day as the young

Turk's birthday: October 31 . . . Halloween.

What all this means is I am now faced with not a choice, but choices. Let me back up a bit here. Six years ago, my second wife and I split up amicably after only 36 months of marriage amidst some serious life choices (there's that word again) that we could not begin to agree upon. But just to give you a hint, she wanted to pursue more of a life in the suburb and grow a family (when we agreed to tie the knot we also made a pact: no children. But she changed her mind!).

She also was pressuring me to leave the novel writing business and to get a real job since I was going through a terrible publishing dry spell. Her parents were relentlessly angry with my decision to continue writing novels, especially after putting up the money for a down payment on a house in the burbs (a down payment and a house I never asked for).

Knowing the situation was impossible, we decided a split would be better now as friends than to have an acrimonious one down the road. However, we shared a daughter who'd become the light of both our lives. Despite my pursuit of all things literary and my itchy desire to travel and gain new experiences both as a journalist and novelist, I wanted that little girl in my life. That in mind, I begged my ex to simply pack up the baby and join me on my adventures. But she would have none of it. So my sons and I left our home, and at her father's insistence, she had the locks changed.

Fast forward six years: Recently, my ex approached me with her desire to pull up stakes and move to California where she would be with her best friend and start a new clothing store. She's unhappy here and desperately wants to get out. Would I stop her from leaving? No, of course not. I just want her to be happy too. Would I follow her there? Would we perhaps reconcile and try to fix our broken relationship?

For a brief moment or two, I actually panicked and at one point broke up with the woman I was seeing since, how could I not follow my ex and our daughter to Cali, even if I have no desire to ever live there? My heartstrings were not being pulled, they were being torn out of my chest.

But then things calmed down, and my girlfriend took me back, and I began to realize that I have no control over my ex and her decisions. I also came to realize that if she wants to pack up and leave that's what she's going to do. My opinion on the matter isn't going to make an ounce of difference. We could always work out visits with our daughter. Heck, perhaps our daughter would like to come live with me at some point. Perhaps spend the summers with me. Time will tell.

But now, I have other things to consider.

My 17 year old son, Harrison (Bear), is still living with me. He's left school in the pursuit of seeing the world and writing his first novel. He will earn his GED, but his desire for a classical education is for now anyway, put on the back burner. I believe he's going to do very well. He has talent. Real God given talent. But much like Larry Darrell in *The Razor's Edge*, he's not at all comfortable with doing things just because you're expected to do them. He needs meaning behind his actions. He needs to know the meaning of life.

So, to make this too long story shorter: I have some choices here. I can either grab a new place to live in the country, further down south but within proximity of where my girlfriend teaches at a local college, so that a train ride to New York is only two hours. Or, I can rent an apartment in New York City where I feel I should be, as a writer. Or, I can move to Europe for a little while which is even further removed from NYC than California, only far way cooler and far less snottier.

In the meantime, Bear and I will head to Italy this week where I've rented an apartment in Florence for the rest of the summer. I need to do a little more research for a couple of novels I'm writing. The good news is that my job allows me to live anywhere that I want. Continued good sales on my books will ensure that. So does my ongoing relationship with my publishers. But the bad news is that choices can be hard to make sometimes. However, it beats the hell out of 9 to 5, work, TV, bed . . . work, TV, bed.

I'm hoping the answer will come to me in Italy next month, maybe while jogging along the Arno in the park, or while sitting outside the Duomo sipping a hot espresso. Or perhaps while climbing some steep terra firma in the Tuscan hills. Perhaps the answer is right before my eyes: a nice place in the country not far from Albany which still places me in excellent proximity to NYC and only 6 hours to Europe.

No matter what decision I make, I will be writing very hard. I'm 47 now, in excellent health, and have reached a point in my life where I have even more time to see the world and to immerse myself in foreign countries and cultures, sort of like the ones I've already experienced in Africa, Russia, Turkey, China, and God knows where. Like Bear, I need to figure out the meaning of life. I need to see the Great Pyramids and Machu Picchu. I need to float down the Amazon in a raft carved from a tree. I want to wander the Saharan desert and I want to go on safari, and I want to photograph the famine in Somalia and perhaps the civil war in Libya. And I want to teach my sons and daughter how to do all of these things too. I want them to know that there is a life outside of the suburbs and that there is real meaning to it. But that life has to be lived before the code can begin to be cracked.

Whether I succeed in doing any of these things will be up to me. The choice is mine. It always has been mine to make. But there is sacrifice in some of these choices. My split from my second wife is perfect evidence of that. But we only go this route once, and we all deserve happiness.

The other day my ex told me she still doesn't know what she wants in life. She's 44 years old and planning a move to the Pacific coast and she doesn't know what she wants. I feel for her. She's not alone. She's a very sweet person and an even sweeter mother. My problem, I told her, is that I've always known precisely what I've wanted out of life. And that can sometimes make a man appear to be selfish. Or why don't I just call it like it is: The pursuit of the perfect life is indeed a selfish pursuit. And yes, at times it feels like I am walking barefoot along the razor's edge. A good life takes great change and choice and sacrifice. But I'll be damned if I can't live any other way.

    —2011

Pieces of Mind

Travels with Myself and Another

I don't often get to travel with my kids. Most of the time, I'm either on assignment or, more accurately, used to be on assignment before I pretty much started back on fiction full time. Or I'm looking for an escape in order to gather inspiration for a new novel. Or I'm simply looking to get the hell out, which is not uncommon for a guy like me who is always itchy (I think I've mentioned before that I never sit down and watch TV, and it's tough to get me to a movie).

So when the opportunity arose to bring my 17 year old son Harrison (we call him Bear) with me to Italy for the month of August for which I've rented an apartment in Florence, Italy, he and I both jumped at the chance. As some of you already know, Harrison is hoping to become a writer and for now anyway, he has traded in his traditional education for one of being self-taught and simply reading and writing (while he pursues a GED).

He also seems to be in search of the meaning of life these days and asking himself questions that many of us either choose to ignore or run away from because they are so dangerous, the most obvious of which is: Am I really happy?

I may not always appear to be the best father to some people, but I know to others I am an exceptional father. I guess I fall somewhere in the middle. My life in unconventional at best but the love I have for my kids can't be defined in terms of convention of mandates, rules and mores or otherwise. It's simply an unconditional love no matter how often or not-so-often I get to see them.

Harrison and I will be living close quarters for the next month in a second floor downtown Florence apartment in a four-hundred year old building, that's spacious and breezy, with plaster walls, exposed wood ceiling beams, tile floors, French windows and doors, and a large terrace that supports an arbor. I will be writing my new novel and reading over the galleys for *Moonlight Rises* and *Scream Catcher* while outlining a new romantic suspense novel based upon one of my most anthologized and translated short stories. We will head to Rome, Pisa and Venice, and we will see the museums and eat the food and drink the drink. But mostly we will spend time together, getting to know one another, as father and son, and as writers.

(To be continued . . .)

Pieces of Mind

—2011

How Art Changes Life

I have been noticing subtle changes in my son Harrison (Bear) as time moves forward during our month-long stay in Florence, Italy. He is not only paying attention to the art and architecture he views for the first time . . . David, Hermes Slays Medusa, the Duomo . . . he is trying to make sense of it all. He finds that the "classic" art has been able to capture the essence of its meaning and in most cases, it is devoid of abstraction. Not a band interpretation for the would-be writer.

Harrison has grown up in a post-post-modern world and is so used to viewing art as an abstraction. Now he is viewing murals and wall paintings that depict "nightmares" so accurately, it's as if he is experiencing them himself.

Today he will see the Uffizi Gallery, the world's most precious collection of Italian art in the world. Giotto, Leonardo, Rubens, Titian, Caravaggio and other masters will peer into Harrison and he will peer into them and his life will be changed even more.

In the process, I get to see how my greatest work of art . . . my son . . . will continue to grow and evolve.

—2011

Father and Son Enjoy a First Beer Together

Ok, comes a time in every parent's life (most parents anyway) where they sit down and enjoy a first beer with their son or daughter. In my case, my son Harrison and I were able to experience exactly that in the Irish Bar located in Santa Maria Novella in Florence, Italy.

Bear is 17 and a half and more than old enough to legally drink a beer here. So what a great opportunity to share something so sacred as a drink with my own son and to unwind and just talk with him in a way we rarely can back in the states.

We took a table outside that my friends who work the establishment cleared for us. The bartender Steve (an art student and all around great dude), brought us two Heineken's a piece. Setting them on the table, Bear grabbed his in his fist and took a big swig. I told him to go easy. The alcohol could go to his head. But he just shrugged his shoulders like, "No big deal, dad."

Suddenly I was reminded of that scene in the 80's comedy classic "Vacation" where Chevy Chase sits down to enjoy a first beer with his teenage son. The kid chugs the beer and crushes the can in his fist, making it plainly apparent it's obviously not his first. Now, I'm not condoning underage drinking here by any means. But what I'm talking about is a sacred rite of passage. In this case, I thought I was above being the forty something naive dad, and totally in tune with my son. But when he downed his beer like it was just another glass of Pepsi,

I knew that this wasn't Bear's first beer by any means.

It made me feel strange, like I didn't know him as well as I should. However, we had one more together and we entered through that rite of passage together and we talked about life and dreams and adventures and ups and downs, and all those things that make up a life worth living.

Sharing your first beer with your son isn't all about beer. It's about love.

—2011

Pieces of Mind

My Son: Chip Off the Old Block . . . Sort Of

Did you ever find yourself watching your teenager eat and whispering softly to yourself: did I eat that much when I was his age?

My 17 year old son, Bear, and I are now entering into week 4 of our month long stay in Italy. All has been smooth sailing as they say thus far, with our having investigated every museum, church, monastery, cathedral, catacomb, and tomb in Rome, Florence and beyond. We've seen relics like bits and pieces of the true cross, pieces of Christ's thorn of crowns, Galileo's teeth and cut off fingers, and the entire mummified body of Cosimo De' Medici (he was a tiny man for having made such a monumental impact on art and architecture). We've climbed mountains, towers and domes, and navigated narrow alleyways and tunnels. We've put in 5 miles a day running along both the Arno and the Tiber and we even found an old gym to bench press and get in some dead-lifting.

All throughout the trip, I could not have asked for a better adventure companion if I'd pre-ordered one from out of an old Montgomery Ward catalog. But I have to say, man, can that boy eat. And not just your average pasta or lasagna. True to form, Bear goes for the more exotic in order to please his palate. Snails drowned in sauce. Squid and muscles soaking in a fish brine. Whole sardines sitting in a vat of olive oil and rank fish heads . . . It seems there is nothing the kid doesn't like or won't try.

I don't recall being that adventurous an eater when I was his age. Pizza mostly, burgers and tacos. That was about the extent of my culinary table of contents. But not the Bear. Like he said on the plane over, he wants to experience everything he can about the life here in Florence.

It's a shame I'm here to work or we might travel to some other out of the way places along the coast. But that will have to wait until I come back in just a few months. In the meantime, Bear wants me to book tickets for us to see the pyramids in Egypt. I'm sure he'll find the pyramids as breathtaking as he did climbing to the cupola atop St. Peter's Cathedral. I'm sure he'll make us ride a camel. He'll want to climb the pyramids, block by solid block. He'll want to look out over the valley and soak it all in.

Afterwards, he'll find something exotic to eat. Something goopy, fishy, rank, and entirely dramatic. Chip off the old block . . . Sort of.

—2011

Finally, the Secret behind Great Sales

A friend of mine who is a published author and great writer just emailed me about what it takes to sell a lot of books. E-Books in particular or so I'm assuming. At first I was ready to dig in with a two page email about marketing and social media and how important it is to maintain a constant presence on these digital mediums. I was also ready to discuss the importance of blogging two or three times a week on topics ranging from how to write a great noir novel to what I did on my summer vacation. Then there's Kindleboards, Goodreads, Crimespace, yadda . . .

But then it occurred to me that no matter how much I talk about these issues, none of them are really responsible for selling books, so much as they simply spread the word about your books being available for sale on the free market. Social media can definitely help you sell books but it can also hurt sales when you abuse and over-use it. After all, you shouldn't be directly selling your books in a social media setting. You should be selling you the human being.

So then, how was it I've been able to sell hundreds of thousands of e-books so far this year?

Jeeze, I'm not entirely sure how I did it.

But I do know this. If you want sell a lot of units (as they are lovingly called in the trade), you need to write great books (luckily my friend has this going for him already). You need a great cover (like me he's traditionally published so he has to rely on his team to produce this for him), a great product description and a very good if not "cheap" yup "cheap" price. As for the rest of the equation, you have to rely on a little luck here.

But then, how can you improve your luck as an author who wants to sell lots of books? The best possible way is simply to write more books. Authors like Scott Nicholson and JA Konrath are making thousands of dollars every month not on just one title, but upwards of 40 titles. These guys aren't sitting on a novel and rewriting it over and over again for two or three years. They are writing them in a matter of two or three months (please don't take this as gospel, I'm merely trying to make a point).

But Vin, you say, how is it possible to write a great novel in two or three months?

My answer is this: can you produce five good pages per day, five days a week? Or are you worried about writers block? If you believe in writers block, you must learn to change your beliefs. Writers block doesn't exist. If you're a writer your job is to show up at work every day and write. Granted, there will be days when Mr. Plot and Mr. Story and Mrs. Brilliance don't show up for work, but that's just the nature of any business. You go with the flow and you keep plugging away anyhow. You take up the slack and plow through the day.

Or here's an idea that might help.

Whenever you feel like it will be impossible to write yet another book, think about your dad or mom. What did they do for a living while they were raising you trying to put clothes on your back, Hamburger Helper on your dinner plate and video games in the Play Station? If your dad was a lawyer, did he ever get lawyer's block? If your mom was a nurse, did you ever hear her complain "I've had absolutely nothing to nurse about for the past six months"? Of course not. Your parents showed up for work five days a week because that was their job. Sometimes it went well, and on occasion, when the proper support staff didn't always show up, things were hard. But by the year's end, they produced a body of work for which they were paid a significant sum.

Back to my point about selling books.

There is no tried or true answer to selling books. Sales flow in cycles. I seem to experience a few weeks of stellar bestselling sales every three or four months or so, probably due to Amazon marketing campaigns. My last great months was in July. I'm not due for another Top 100 Kindle Bestseller months until October or November. But then, this is just a guestimate. I have no control over Amazon marketing, other than signing on with their publisher, Thomas and Mercer, which I'm about to do.

So, in the final analysis, there is only one tried and true method of increasing your chances of selling books. That tried and true method is to show up for work every day, and write more of them.

—2011

Vincent Zandri

"You'll Never Get a Major Deal Again!"

"You'll never get a major deal again!"

Sounds harsh doesn't it. Even cruel, especially when it comes from the mouth of a respected independent bookstore owner who operates one of the most successful bookselling operations out of Albany.

This was the scene: a year ago or so, said bookstore owner was lamenting the fact that my newest novel at the time, *The Remains*, was being published in trade paper and E-Book by an indie press. Due to the slowdown in paper sales because of E-Book sales and other economic factors, she didn't want to take the book on in the traditional manner by ordering it from the distributor. She wanted it on consignment. That way she wouldn't get burned down the road by having to hang on to unsold books.

When I explained to her that she could by all means return the books, she wouldn't hear of it. Ok, fair enough. These are trying economic times after all, and book stores are quickly going the way of the record store and the Blockbuster video store. Somehow our talk shifted to my original major deal with two Random House imprints back in '99 and 2000. I mentioned how my agent was going after another major deal based on the excellent E-Book sales I'd been experiencing thus far with *The Remains*. That's when she turned to me, looked me in the eye and said, "Vincent, you will never get a major deal again!" It wasn't like a slap to the face, it was more like a swift kick to the soft underbelly. She then backed up her statement by telling me the deal with RH had been fluke. The editors were tossing major six-figure deals around like confetti back then. Didn't matter the talent or the inherent value of the writing.

Wow, if I didn't already feel poorly enough about having to be on consignment at her shop, now I was made to feel like a total loser. I mean, I thought bookstore owners were supposed to prop up writers? Work with them? Live in harmony? You need me and I need you and all that . . .

Fast forward a few months.

The Innocent, Godchild and *The Remains* all hit the Top 100 on Amazon Kindles and eventually the Top 20. I started moving around 3,000 units per day. That's right. That's not a typo. 3,000 units. *The Innocent* hit the Top 10 and stayed there for seven weeks. In the meantime, I completed yet another novel,

Murder by Moonlight. My agent wanted to go out to sale with it, hoping for the major deal said bookstore owner claimed would be impossible.

The Big 6 in New York all enthusiastically expressed interest in getting a read. So did another major publisher. A new major publisher that's emerged from out of Amazon. Thomas and Mercer. I'd heard about this publisher as not a major in the traditional sense, but more of a hybrid indie and major in which the author receives a terrific E-book royalty on top of being published in hardcover, audio and trade, and along with it, a nice advance or even better.

What makes this new publisher more enticing than the Big 6 however, is their direct connection to Amazon, the biggest store in the world. This publisher will not only sell your books but it is in their best interest to market them and even position them to sell. Something the Big 6 cannot guarantee.

I told my agent that if we did indeed get an offer from T&M that I wouldn't entertain a Big 6 deal, even if they offered me a much larger advance. I wanted to be at a home that represented the future of book selling. I wanted a place that would offer me security and a voice as an author. T&M, I was told would offer that and more. Then, when I heard that big name bestsellers like JA Konrath and Barry Eisler were signing contracts with T&M, that entirely iced the deal for me.

Just yesterday my agent excitedly forwarded my new contract from T&M to me for my review. There's a few details we're ironing out, but it looks great. I'm not at liberty to discuss the upfront money or the percentages, but suffice to say I'm back in the big leagues in a big way. Not only is T&M publishing *Murder by*

Moonlight, but they are re-publishing five titles on my back-list, including *The Innocent* and *The Remains*—a first for my agent who has been in the publishing business for two decades. News will be forthcoming in all the usual trades: PW, etc. It's an exciting time for me and my entire family.

"You will never get a major deal again!" said the bookstore owner.

Sometimes I love proving people wrong.

—2011

Is Rejection Good for You?

There's been a lot of chatter lately about the e-Book market being flooded with crappy books from writers who would, under traditional publishing circumstances, not only be rejected by major publishers but also by most discerning agents. In other words, their writing sucks. But being able to publish your own book these days means you don't have to go through the often terrible trials that most editors can put upon a budding author by lambasting said literary neophyte with rejection after rejection.

Like my dad always says, "But that's the job."

I entered into the literary arena as a traditionalist back in the early '90s,

261

having started out at a local newspaper, then working my way up to regional magazines, and eventually national publications. I wrote my first publishable short story in 1991 after four or five years of writing nothing that was publishable. Or, at least, nothing that was ever accepted by a decent literary magazine or journal. Then I went to writing school where I began my first full-length novel that was to become *As Catch Can* and later, *The Innocent.* It sold to Delacorte almost immediately upon my graduation and for a time, it looked like rejection, and the ugly horse she road in on, was a thing of the past. Forever.

Then came the dismantling of my publishing house, and *Catch* was largely forgotten about. I published one more novel with the biggies, *Godchild,* but by then, the Big 6 were already entering into a tailspin of consolidation and house cleaning. Having earned a major six-figure advance I was now out on my ass as they say, and only as good as my next manuscript.

I wrote that manuscript and while my agent loved it, it was rejected by the big six. So I wrote another one. That one got rejected. It wasn't the quality of the writing I was told, it was my having not earned out my advance. But that wasn't my fault I bellowed. No one wanted to hear it. My argument was rejected.

Still I labored on, and wrote yet one more novel. Same story. No one would take me on.

In the meantime, other forms of rejection awaited me. Friends rejected me for being down in the dumps. My max'ed out credit cards rejected me. My emptying bank accounts rejected me. A good night's sleep rejected me. Health rejected me. My ability to quit smoking rejected me (I've since been smoke free for 6 years, but bear with me) Even my new lovely wife, who was growing impatient with my inability to make a living, rejected the crap out of me. So did her family. They wanted me to give up full-time writing and go to work for my dad's business, whom I had worked for in the past while honing my skills. Problem was, if I worked full-time, I couldn't write. And I knew in my heart that the only way to break through the hell-hole of rejection was to write. Not write "on the side" as some of them were saying.

So I persevered, even when my wife divorced me. My life might have entered into a tailspin of rejection and humiliation for a year or so, but always, the writing was my constant. It was the light I could rely upon in the midst of all that darkness.

When *Moonlight Falls* got accepted by a small press, and did very well I was elated. Later when *The Remains* was accepted by an indie publisher and produced as an e-Book first, I was entirely skeptical that anything good could come out of it. I had no idea about e-Books and initially rejected the notion that they would replace paper as the dominant manner of reading. But when it eventually hit the Top 100 and then the Top 20, I was hooked.

You would think that I might cut the cord at that point, and kick rejection in the ass and simply self-publish from that point forward. But something in my gut told me to continue with the traditional route. The process, while grueling and often times frustrating, still worked for me. Which is why I prefer to continue working with an agent who reads my manuscripts first for their quality and promise. Later on, my publisher will do the very same thing. If they reject it, there's probably a good reason. You know, like it sucks or something (Luckily this hasn't happened yet . . . I'm on a roll as they say).

Now I'm signing a 7 book deal with Thomas & Mercer, potentially the biggest powerhouse publisher on the block. I have many more novels in me that will have to be read by my agent first and then my editor at T&M. Even though I could simply publish the novels myself, I choose to go this route and risk being rejected yet again.

Why?

Because for me . . . and I speak only for me . . . risking rejection makes me a better writer. And it's more important for me to have a reader tell me *Concrete Pearl* or *Scream Catcher* was "brilliantly written," than to be in the Amazon Top 10. Ok, well, I lie, that rocks too (*The Innocent* graced the Top 10 for 7 weeks . . .). But if I'm going to be a writer who not only has staying power, but whose audience continues to grow and expand all over the globe, then every now and then, a little ass kicking might do me some good.

—2011

Pieces of Mind

The Most Selfish Occupation on Earth

My ex-wife (the second one) used to call me selfish. She claimed my work came before my family. That all the hours I put into my writing was taking away from the quality time I might otherwise share with she and the kids. Which I never quite understood since I usually never work nights and was often the Johnny-on-the-spot when it came to making dinners, feeding the crew and helping out with the homework. You know, domestic stuff like that. My ex was pretty good at making reservations. That was about it. Ok, I'm joking. In her defense she worked and took care of quite a few household chores that might have otherwise never gotten done. Like the laundry for instance.

But in terms of work, I was not only diligent, I often worked seven days a week writing and marketing my novels. I recall a time when guests of hers were over and she simply introduced me as her husband. When the topic of writers and books came up, it struck me as odd and frankly, kind of sad, that she never once uttered a word about my being a published novelist. Later on, the when the guests were gone, I asked her why she did that. Her response was, 'You already have enough of an ego.' Can you just see the steam pouring out of my ears??????

I guess by then the marriage was over (all 36 months of it) and by that time, she'd had enough of the importance I placed on my writing and the sacrifices we all had to make in order to see a novel become a success. I can't say I blame her.

However, I will say that she knew what she was getting into, since when I met her I was a novelist and when we married I remained a novelist (despite her family insisting I get a "real job in the real world.")

There's a reason why many successful authors tend to marry and divorce several times over. The reason is simple: Our work is indeed the most important thing in our lives. Doesn't mean we don't love our kids and spoil them and dote over them. Doesn't mean I didn't love my wife. I loved her to death. But the fact is, when it came to my work schedule, nothing was going to get in the way of it. Not chores, not social engagements, not sickness, not even Christmas. Work isn't even the word for writing. It's more of a calling, a devotion to a religion. Or, maybe this will make more sense to you in a down-to-earth-way: A farmer has to get up and milk the cows and feed the chickens on Christmas morning just like any other day. The animals don't know the difference. The farmer isn't working. He's living a lifestyle and adhering to a calling that is far different from the usual 9-5, sleep, TV, bed that most people are used to. That's the precise allure of the job, no matter how hard and grueling it can be.

I guess when people get married, they see themselves changing their partner's ways and habits to a certain extent. They envision a spouse who will be more sensitive to their needs and wants, and this can include time set aside for them. Nothing wrong with this so long as a fine balance is maintained and said spouse doesn't go overboard with the changes she intends to pursue in her man (and vice/versa naturally). But what she should realize prior to walking down that aisle is that she is marrying a writer. An artist. She is marrying someone who is indeed selfish and self-centered and full of ego. Because that's precisely what it takes to make it as a writer. It is a selfish occupation that will often cause you to lose not only marriages, but relationships and friendships of all kinds, and you, as an aspiring published author, must be prepared for that.

Hemingway went through four wives, and many friends. But his writing was his constant. So long as he could write, his reason for living was intact. Nothing could interfere with it, and nothing would ever stand in its way. And when the words would no longer come to him, he enacted the most selfish act of all. His fourth wife Mary woke up and found his slumped over body in the vestibule of their Ketchum, Idaho home, and what was left of his brains spattered against the walls. Norman Mailer married eight times,

Michael Crichton eight times, Stephen
Crane eight times, and the list goes on
and on.

I'm not trying to portray a dismal
picture here. I'm trying to be honest. As
full-time writers who wish to work alone
for hours at a time but who also wish to
engage in meaningful relationships, there
will come a time sooner than later that we
will be accused of being selfish and full of
ego. We will be accused of placing more
importance on our work than we do on
our children and our spouses. Even when
we have become successful we will still
crave attention and affirmation like a
spoiled child screaming out behind a
locked bedroom door. And we will want to
continue to work harder than ever before.

But if you can somehow strike a
balance between the work and the ego,
and your loved one's needs and wants
while still achieving great success, you will

be the luckiest person alive. I've yet to find a way to strike that balance and it's cost me dearly. But I'm thankful for what I've achieved and I'm always hopeful that one day, that delicate balance will come before it's too late. For now anyway, I'd better get back to work.

—*2011*

Pieces of Mind

Winners Never Quit!

You've heard the old saying so many times you probably wanna hurl when you see it: Winners never quit and quitters never win.

It was true back when I was playing high school football and it's still true today. Never more so than in the independent writing world. I read recently that many of the authors (up to 98% of them) who are now turning their backs on rejection for the freedom and ease of independent publishing via Amazon and other similar digital e-Book DIY programs, will eventually quit. And I mean, quit within a year of their entry into independent publishing.

Why?

Because they won't sell. Or, wait, scratch that. It's not that they won't sell, it's that they will perceive themselves as not selling. It's no surprise that many of these would-be authors took one look at the John Locke's of the indie publishing world and said to themselves, "Well, hell, I can do that." They logged onto Amazon KDP, downloaded their book, slapped a cover onto it, priced it at $.99 and watched it crash in the rankings like the Hindenburg into New Jersey.

"Oh, the humanity . . ."

What happened here?

The instant success that these authors feel was warranted in the face of constant rejection, in the face of having to get up for a job they hate, in the face of writing friends who are becoming a success, in the face of that awful dark thing that fills your head at night when you lay it down on your pillow, just didn't arrive. At least not right away.

But what these quitters do not see is the light at the end of the publishing tunnel. Instead of writing more books and publishing those, they will give up on indie publishing and go back to seeking out a traditional deal, which in this day and age is becoming a near impossibility, unless you are already showing some great success in the indie publishing world. See how that works now????

For those of you committed to indie publishing no matter your sales; for those of you thinking long term; for those of you who understand that success at this thing takes time, and hitting your stride in the marketplace takes even more time and persistence, never fear. Most of the authors whom you are competing against in the indie marketplace won't be here next year. It will be the good authors who never quit who will eventually become the successes and the full-time writers.

The quitters will get up on a bone cold, dark, unforgiving morning, fire up a cigarette, and head out to work.

—*2011*

In the Fall of the Year. Or, The Path Not Taken

My brief ten day hiatus from the blogosphere is now officially over. My thanks to the guest bloggers who more than took up the slack. You enabled me to get through the new draft of *BLUE MOONLIGHT* (the sequel to the newly released *MOONLIGHT RISES*) while offering some sage advice on writing, marketing, and just living the literary life in this the digital age.

I'm calling this "In the Fall of Year . . . " because even though Fall is my favorite season by far, it seems always to accompany serious change in my life and in some cases, downright turmoil. Maybe the Fall is actually no different from any other season, but that it just seems more intense since this is the time when I am at my most creative. What did Hemingway once say about the Fall: That's the time when real writers put pen to paper. But I also think it has something to do with the proximity of death in that whole the Fall-leads-to-Winter notion of the idea.

Since my return from Europe in September I've realized several ends and even more beginnings. As for the former, my relationship with my girlfriend came to a final end, and as for the former, my son Harrison was able to take his GED exam (he assumes he passed). Now he can begin his work as a writer and video game designer in earnest. Such are his plans. His brother Jack will turn 21 in two weeks, and it will certainly be interesting, to say the least, to view my son as an adult, rather than a kid. While my brief foray into the world of independent publishing comes not to a full closure, but rather that of a transition back into traditional publishing, I find myself at a cross-roads.

Do I remain in Albany, and continue to forge ahead with a life here? Or, at 47, do I look for a new place to begin again? Even if it's only thirty miles away. Final destination possibilities abound inside my skull like those steel ball-bearings that bounce against the insides of a spray paint can. At one minute I'm thinking New York City while the very next, I'm thinking Florence, Italy, full-time. Both are expensive these days, so I'm also thinking somewhere out west like Boise, but then I'll look at a small Hudson River town not far south from where I live now and I think, Yah, that's the ticket . . . Small town living while remaining in the general proximity of Manhattan and just 6 hours to Europe.

Whether I move or not, the point is not location, but transition. We all need to recognize when our entire being requires a tune-up and the best time for that is during these transitional phases. Who wants to be that fat guy sitting on the couch watching reality TV with a beer in hand chanting, "Shoulda, Coulda, Woulda . . .?"

Well, first of all I don't watch reality TV and second of all, I don't even own a TV any longer. But as we age, life becomes a slippery slope, and next thing you know, you've just spent the airline ticket money on a new LCD and a satellite hookup. Welcome to soft middle age.

This has been one of the best years of my life in terms of career, creativity, travel, and attempting to piece together this life that I have stubbornly built for myself. The transition isn't over yet by a long shot. But sooner than later, I will be

forced to make a few hard decisions and
once their made, I'm going to have to stick
to them.

Now that's the scary part about life.
Sticking to your decisions once you've
made them.

—*2011*

Pieces of Mind

The Cards You Have Been Dealt

Five years ago I thought my novelist days were over.

My two-book contract with Random House had not been renewed after I didn't earn out a mid-six-figure advance. I had no prospect of publishing with a new major publisher since leaving six-figures on the table was tantamount to career suicide. I could no longer afford my house, or my Jeep. My wife, who married me when things were going great in the literary life, no longer felt so eager to be married to a man who couldn't get his third book published, even after we'd just had a child together. In her defense, we were hitting financial rock bottom.

While her family was screaming at me (sometimes literally) to "get a job" and "write on the side," they had also begun to initiate the process over which my wife would eventually cave in. Her family made her a deal she couldn't refuse: leave the bum and we'll take care of you. Buy you a new house, pay for your living expenses, help you raise your daughter.

My wife was left with a difficult choice to make. Stick with her husband and soul mate, and work through this very hard period, or choose to side with her family. She chose the latter. In doing so she played her hand, cashed in her chips, and removed herself from the gaming table. But at least she became financially stable again and wasn't even required to get a job in order to maintain her bank account.

I too chose not to get a job, but to stay the course of the writer. However, the hand I'd been dealt didn't look too sweet. It consisted of a whole lot of low cards with a couple of jokers tossed in. But there was nothing left for me but to stay the course no matter how bleak the future. I'd lost my wife, my child, my house, my money, and possibly, my career. You'd think I'd lose my sanity at the same time? But writing was my sanity, and it was my solace and my art, and no amount of outside pressure was going to extinguish the fire that burned from within. Call it stubbornness in the face of absolute calamity. Call it stupidity. Call it what you will. But like the bulldog that gets its arm stuck in the trap, I'd rather chew it off then die on someone else's terms.

So what did I do?

I downsized. I rented a 900 sq.ft. apartment with my two sons, and decided to start all over again. In other words, I didn't fold my cards, but instead, decided to persist at the gaming table and play them no matter how much bluffing and game-facing it was going to take. Curiously, in the immediate wake of my marital demise, doors started opening for me. I went back to freelance journalism, and began to build up a cache of published articles, professional blogs, global assignments and a new reputation as a foreign correspondent and photo-journalist. Within a year of splitting with my wife, I found myself on assignment in Africa, Moscow, Italy, Spain and other exotic locales. I was living and working in places like Florence, Italy for up to a month at a time, and making money at it. I became happy, but I also became a bit perplexed. Why wasn't I able to take advantage of these working opportunities when I was married? What was it about the marriage that made it impossible for me to succeed? Were the two related, or was my new found success in the absence of marriage entirely a coincidence?

While my non-fictional life regained momentum, I also went back to serious fiction writing. I wrote *MOONLIGHT FALLS*, *THE REMAINS*, *CONCRETE PEARL*, and *PATHOLOGICAL*, all within a 36 month period. I found a new agent who loved my previously published work and the new work even more, and who committed herself to finding me a new home, even if that new home were a smaller press than I was used to. In terms of playing my hand, it wasn't a matter of walking away with the entire the pot at this point, it was a matter of getting back into the game and staying there, improving my hand the entire time with each and every ante.

Things happened. Good things.

I contracted with a small press for *MOONLIGHT FALLS*. Despite all expectations, and a new-found appreciation for social media marketing and virtual tours, it hit the hard-boiled bestseller list on Amazon and stayed there. It was my first experience ever being a bestseller of any kind. That one experience led to a new contract for *THE REMAINS*. One which caught me off guard. Up until a few years ago, I really had no idea what an E-Book was. But my agent was so excited about the new opportunities in this medium that she could hardly express herself without hyperventilating. She informed me that she was about to strike up a new deal with a new publisher out of Boise of all places. A new young, maverick indie publisher who was making waves in the industry by publishing mid and back-listers like me, who although previously published by major houses, had found themselves treading water in a purgatorial sea of uncertainty, disbelief and utter terror at what the future might hold.

The indie publisher would publish *THE REMAINS* in E-Book first and then paper. Which at the time, I thought was *bass-ackwards*. Paper always comes out first, followed by the e-book and audio. My agent persevered and asked me to give it a try. There'd be no advance, but I would be offered instead a 50% royalty rate on all E-Books sold. What's more, the book would be released within two months from contract execution. Something unheard of in traditional legacy publishing realms. Believing the whole endeavor would crash and burn, I nonetheless trusted my agent, and said to myself, "What the hell!" I anted up, and stayed in the game deciding to keep on playing the new cards I'd been dealt.

Then something wonderful happened.

I not only hit the bestseller list in Hard-Boiled Mystery. But I hit the Romantic Suspense and Psychological Thriller lists as well. The numbers kept improving. Encouraged, the indie publisher started a new imprint for hard-boiled writers like myself. They published my former Random House books, *THE INNOCENT* and *GODCHILD*, now that the publishing rights had been released. These books would go on within six months of E-Book publication to not only make their respective bestseller lists, but to hit the overall Amazon Kindle Bestseller Lists, not just in North America, but in several European countries as well. In fact, *THE INNOCENT* would go on to grace the Kindle Top Ten Overall Bestseller's list for 7 weeks, and the Top 100 for almost 20 weeks. At one point I was selling 3,000 E-Books per day and moving more units than Stephen King. In the end, *"Innocent"* sold over 100,000 copies during the Spring rush. Within five years of contemplating cashing it all in and folding my cards, I'd become an International Bestseller. Poor Random House. If only they'd had faith that my books had the potential not only to earn out my six-figure advance but also to make a nice tidy profit, they might have kept on publishing me instead of remaindering all of my work and holding the rights hostage for ten years.

That was five months ago. Things haven't been the same since.

The most dramatic change has been the new cards I've been dealt. I've now signed a new lucrative contract with the renegade Amazon powerhouse publisher, Thomas & Mercer, the major player who is publishing not only my new novel, *Murder By Moonlight*, but nearly my entire back-list. But that doesn't mean I can't maintain my relationship with other publishers and continue to publish as an independent. It also means I will continue my work as a journalist and an explorer. Because in the end, I've learned, it's not the cards you have in your hand, it's how you play them. It's also a matter perseverance, a steadfast belief in one's self and one's talents, and an ability to keep on working even during some of the most tumultuous, depressing, and indeed, angering times you will ever experience in a single lifetime. It means developing the skills never to be defeated and to grow stronger in the broken places.

This past weekend, my ex-wife and I took our six year old daughter for a ride out in the country to pick out pumpkins and apples. It was a bright sunny Fall afternoon on the Upstate New York/New England border with the leaves on the trees having turned all shades of brilliant red, orange and yellow. One of those days where you can get away with either a sweater or a light jacket. We spent the day as if we were a tight knit family. And in a way are tightly knit and certainly even closer than some marriages that exist in a state of siege. My ex and I were able to look into one another's eyes and realize that all the anger over what happened when my career temporarily tanked is past. There remains now only our child and bringing her up knowing that she has two parents who love her and who will be there for her thick or thin. No amount of literary success or sales can ever replace that.

But I recognize a distinct sadness in my ex-wife's eyes now when I peer into them. I believe the sadness is wrought over something that could never be changed or reversed once it was put in place by the very same people who were once responsible for her wellbeing as a child and adolescent. Her adult life decisions and the effect it has had on her now as a middle aged woman ring out and reverberate with an irony so intense, it is both deafening and bone shattering.

But my ex-wife and I, we are no better than anyone else. Life isn't exactly fair. You win some and you lose some. But one thing however is for certain: we, as writers, are all victims of our desires, slaves to love, and powerless in the face of blind passion. We are artists and we are as much blessed by God as we are doomed by the fallen angels.

My ex-wife and I still love one another. We often remind each other of it. Many times I don't get off the phone with her without saying, "Love you." But we cannot have one another any longer. Perhaps it's too late to rekindle embers that have not only grown cold, but have disintegrated and seeped into the earth over the course of the many seasons. But if we are the least bit intelligent, we have both learned a vital lesson five years in the making. When you're dealt a hand of cards and you are forced to make the final decision on whether to stay in the game no matter the quality of the hand, or to fold them and walk away from the table, the decision better be the right one. Because when the time comes for the great dealer in the sky to make His call, and all bets are suddenly off, you will be left alone with your choice, right or wrong.

That choice had better come straight from the heart, because it will be something you must live with for the rest of your life.

—2011

Pieces of Mind

Love Stinks

I write a lot about love.

I can't avoid it.

In any given story there's got to be a love element. Whether it's about falling in love, or out of love, or about avoiding love for a moment or two of lust, which can be lovely but entirely devoid of being in love . . . if you catch my drift.

Bear with me here.

Truth be told, I'm a total sap. So what that means is, I'm especially attracted to those stories that not only pit one man against the world, but that also contain an almost impossible to fulfill love story. You know, the stories about unrequited love, or love that's crushed due to vast distances in geography, time, or space. Then there's the love and war stories that made Papa so famous, and even the Hammett-style hard-boiled drama of the private detective who falls in love with the "dame" who turns out to be a black window. In the end he's got no choice but to watch her being carted away to jail while he flips up the collar on his leather coat, lights a cigarette with his Zippo, and walks away from it all in the rain-soaked neon lit darkness. If you've never read my noir novels, it's the latter image of love-gone-wrong that you will inevitably receive.

Romantic?

Yes.

Realistic . . . Even more yes.

I'm one of those authors who like Hemingway or Mailer likes to taut the tough guy image in his main characters (even if the main character is a woman like in *CONCRETE PEARL*). But I also like to show off their sensitive side. Mostly I do this by proving how prone they are to falling head over heels for someone (as opposed to heels over head). They don't just love with a logical perspective attached to the emotion. They love until it hurts; until they can't sleep or eat or function as a productive human being. In a word, they suffer love so much that they are reduced to a sweat-soaked bundle of or rags and bones. When these ill-fated characters are separated from their love interests by either geography or breakup, their imaginations play evil tricks in them. So evil that Richard "Dick" Moonlight, anti-hero of my Moonlight series, once placed a .22 caliber revolver to his head, and pulled the trigger.

That "Love is Kind" Bible passage that always gets read at weddings is pure bullshit.

Love isn't kind.

Love stinks.

Love hurts.

Love sneaks up on you when you least expect it.

Love is not friendly.

Love is like water torture.

Love will drive you to drink.

Love causes suicide.

Love sucks.

But for some reason, love is what we all crave and live for.

Falling hopelessly in love is unbearable. Especially when you find someone whom you've been searching for your whole life and by reasons of timing or commitment to another, can't quite as easily give the love back. Even if she wants to more than anything in the world.

Such is life.

Such is romance.

Such is Cupid's painfully sharp arrow.

—2011

A Few More Minutes with Andy Rooney

I'm having a trouble imagining a world without Andy Rooney. It's kind of like trying to imagine Star Wars without Yoda. How else are we supposed to move on with our lives while having to put up with its everyday absurdities, banalities, and garden variety foolery? Did I just write the word "foolery"?

Andy worked almost right up until the end. As writers we never retire. But he did give up the TV gig with *60 Minutes* only a month ago, which should serve as a sort of be a warning to those seniors who insist on working well into their golden years. Don't give up the day job!

I can just picture this week's *A Few Minutes With Andy Rooney* if only we were to be graced with one more. He'd appear in the crumpled up suit he pulled out from under his bed, even though God would probably offer him a nicer choice of threads. He might look a little younger, maybe because he wouldn't be in pain. Old age is often accompanied by aches and pains. He might bear a little more of a smile. His eyebrows might be trimmed. But I think otherwise, he'd be the same old crotchety Andy. The subject of his spot would be "Retiring."

"It's not retiring that's hard," he'd write. "It's the dying part of retirement that is."

He might say that had he known he was gonna cash it all in within a month of retirement, he would have negotiated a better end-of-career bonus with the network. He would have coined this as a

"Sure to Perish Immediately Upon Retirement" clause or something like that. Then he might have mentioned other famous men and women who have "retired" and died soon after. Since I can't think of anyone famous who has died very soon after quitting their job, I can tell you that I've had a couple of uncles who retired from the construction business and died within a year or so. It's a warning for my dad who at 76 is still putting in a full week. Keep working!!!

Andy was an everyman's writer in that he didn't believe in writer's block any more than a plumber believes in plumber's block. He once wrote: "Writers are repeatedly asked to explain where they get their ideas. People want their secret. The truth is there is no secret and writers don't have many new ideas. At least, they don't have many ideas that a comic strip artist would illustrate with a light bulb over their heads."

Andy's ideas came from the everyday. Like procrastinating before getting to work. Or having to deal with pulling out all that cotton filling in your plastic bottle of Advil. Once he wrote about how the French had expelled something like 47 then Soviet spies that year from France. "That's a lot of spies," he wrote.

I mean, how can you not smile and laugh a little on the inside when you read that?

I've met Andy on a few occasions, most of them having to do with a private high school we both attended up in Albany called The Albany Academy. I attended the place in the 80s and Andy in the 30s. The place has changed a lot in the many years since I moped around its marble halls. But back in the early 80s it wasn't much different than the school that Andy attended. It was a military country day prep school that prided itself on discipline as much as it did sports and the arts. We wore military uniforms and ate not in a cafeteria, but a "buttery." Also, Andy played left guard for the football team and so did I. We played the same position and we were both under five feet, eight inches. We took a lot of pounding in those four years, but we gave a lot out too. Maybe that's why we became writers. All that head banging will prevent you from looking at the world in a conventional way.

I guess I've known Andy my whole life, having first taken notice of him when *60 Minutes* would pop on the TV after the New York Giants football games. Even if we were bummed out about the Giants losing a barn burner to the rival Dallas Cowboys in the last minute of the last quarter, and even if we were in a black mood over having to go to school or work in the morning, we could always count on Andy gracing the screen in his wrinkled suit. You'd wait for the topic of his "few minutes" with baited breath. When finally he'd come out with something like, "It costs us almost a quarter for every mile we drive a car," we knew we were in for something special about something not so special. And that getting up in the morning and putting on your socks one at a time, wasn't all that different from the life he was living. Andy was just a regular guy in possession of an extraordinary talent.

I'm going to miss Andy Rooney and his words and his unconventional wisdom about the conventional. I'm going to miss running into him and having to remind him of my name and what I do for a living. That stuff never bothered me because I was such a fan with a little hero worship sprinkled in. Did you know that during World War II Andy spent about an hour hiding in a ditch alongside a road that had been strafed by German planes along with Ernest Hemingway? How many people can brag about something like that? But Andy would be the last guy on earth to talk about Papa. He'd be more apt to comment on how every buffet you dine at no matter how nice the facility always offers you Swedish meatballs. He'd write about how you couldn't resist the Swedish meatballs even after some of the gravy got on your tie and stained it. He'd show up on TV the next week with the same tie and the same stain. It would become a heated topic of discussion. A philosophy. A reason to carry on in the everyday.

Enjoy the afterlife Andy.

Keep writing.

Keep being you.

—2011

Pieces of Mind

No Rest for the Weary . . .

I'm tired.

Beat.

Ripped to shreds.

Tossing in the towel.

Asleep on the feet . . .

I can't believe I just wrote all that.
But it's true. I think by now you know me
as this unstoppable writer guy who can't
sit still for more than the few hours it
takes every day to write his five pages.
Invincible Vince, as it were. But since I got
back from Europe a couple of months ago
I've been undergoing some tremendous life
changes, the least of which is signing the
new deal for two new books and five
backlist books with Thomas &
Mercer/Amazon and also not the least of
which is my oldest son's 21st birthday.

Life is different for me now in that I'm contemplating a change of living venue . . . a new heaven on earth. And even though I haven't quite figured out where I will call home over the next six months (whether it will be the US or Europe or both), I can tell that I'm now completing a life phase that includes the completion of four books, four short stories, and articles/blogs too numerous to count in the past five years. It also includes travels . . . travels encompassing Africa to Moscow and L.A. to Italy, sometimes for a weeks at a time.

These are just the things I can tell you. Because there are also things happening in my life that I can't quite reveal yet, although I will one day when it's right (It could be months from now!). I know, I know . . . I know what you're thinking. Don't be keeping secrets from inquiring minds. But let's put it this way. I haven't actually been "in love" (I mean real, gut wrenching love) in quite some time and it's possible that where ever I do decide to lay my head, she will be there with me . . . Enough said on that subject.

Back to business . . .

But now that I've signed my contracts, I've felt a wave of exhaustion and emotion pour over me like a waterfall. This isn't an unusual experience. Often when I complete a novel, I find myself sleeping more than I do spending awake time. It's not an unusual reaction to a job well done.

So what's my point?

I'm always preaching to my peeps to get those pages done, put ass cheeks to the chair cushion, ignore the world and write your pages. But, and this is a big BUT, when your body begins to send you signs that you need to take some time off and relax, don't ignore them. For me, the signs are attention deficit, trembling hands, lack of appetite, upset stomach, inability to enjoy the foods I normally enjoy, night terrors, melancholy, bi-polar like mood swings, and just a desperate need to get some serious sleep.

Or . . . wait a minute . . . Hold the freakin' phone . . . Maybe I'm fooling myself here. Maybe there's nothing wrong with my writing or work/travel schedule. Maybe all these "signs" as it were have nothing to do with too much on my work plate. After all, writing isn't just a job for me. It's a passion and a hobby and a religion all mixed up together. Maybe they have everything to do with something else. Maybe, just maybe, I've fallen in love again . . .

—2011

Renewing Your Writer Vows

I've experienced one of the hardest seven days of my life this past week with the unexpected and very sudden death of my dad who dropped dead while tying his shoes after having jogged his daily three miles and having gotten in a full free-weights workout. Being in the possession of a strong heart, even at 76 years of age, he over exerted himself on this particular morning and his heart stopped. No resuscitation possible, despite a valiant effort on the part of EMTs who worked on his chest for nearly an hour. By the time he arrived at the hospital in Albany he was DOA.

My dad was a giver and he liked to be involved even if in a small way in all the lives of his children and grandchildren. He was also a control man who liked to do things his way, and his way only. So now that he is suddenly gone, I find myself wanting to give him a call regarding matters that have to do entirely with him. The paradox is heartbreaking.

Despite the tragedy of his sudden death, I am nonetheless a better man for it in that I have had a lot of growing up to do this week, not the least of which is deciding how I am going to handle the next thirty to forty years of my life. How I can carry on in a way that will make him proud. Curiously, I find myself looking at my writing in a new light. I find myself wanting to work even harder and better than ever. That means slowing down on certain projects in order to grab the most meaning out of the fewest words possible. It will take concentration and a renewed effort.

I also find myself more committed to traveling to some of those exotic destinations I have not yet experienced. Borneo, Tibet, Mongolia . . . and beyond. Life is a process and like a story it has a beginning, a middle and an end. Often times we don't know when that end will occur. It can come when you least expect it, like when you're tying your shoes for instance. It's your responsibility to live that life to the fullest in the meantime. And living life means discovering things. The world is out there. Go walk it. And while you're doing that, work hard. Very hard.

Starting Monday, I am renewing my writing vows so that I can hit the New Year in full sprint. You should too. Here's how I'm going to conduct my days:

—Get out of bed by 7AM, and be at my writing desk with coffee in hand by 7:15

—I will write 2 to 3 pages in the morning (or if editing, 10 to 15 pages)

—At around 10:30, I'll go for a run and hit the gym.

—By 1:30, I'll be back at my desk for another 2-3 pages.

—When that's done, I'll put in an hour or so of marketing via the social networks and my blog.

—On Saturdays, I will work in the mornings and take the afternoon off.

—Sundays are days off (unless I have a deadline looming).

I'm going to commit myself to this routine even when traveling, so long as it's possible (I understand it's pretty hard to write sentences on your laptop from up on a camel's back). I think my dad would be proud to hear that I'm renewing my writing vows. Every day he got up, put on his running shoes and hit the pavement in

the dark and cold of the dawn, and then
he showered up and went off to work.
Nothing stopped him from doing what he
needed to do for himself and for those
around him whom he loved and who
depended upon him. He worked to both
please himself and to make the world
know that he was here, if only for a brief
but poignant time.

—2011

Join Vincent Zandri's "For Your Eyes Only" mailing list for monthly giveaways, contests, book announcements, and other cool stuff. Just go to

http://www.vincentzandri.com

About the Author

Winner of the 2015 PWA Shamus Award and the 2015 ITW Thriller Award for Best Original Paperback Novel for *MOONLIGHT WEEPS*, Vincent Zandri is the *NEW YORK TIMES, USA TODAY*, and *AMAZON KINDLE* No.1 bestselling author of more than 25 novels including *THE REMAINS, EVERYTHING BURNS, ORCHARD GROVE* and *THE CORRUPTIONS*. He is also the author of numerous Amazon bestselling digital shorts, *PATHOLOGICAL* and *DOG DAY MOONLIGHT* among them. Harlan Coben has described *THE INNOCENT* (formerly *As Catch Can*) as " . . . gritty, fast-paced, lyrical and haunting," while the New York Post called it "Sensational . . . Masterful . . . Brilliant!" Zandri's list of domestic publishers include

Delacorte, Dell, Down & Out Books, Thomas & Mercer, and Polis Books. An MFA in Writing graduate of Vermont College, Zandri's work is translated in the Dutch, Russian, French, Italian, and Japanese. Recently, Zandri was the subject of a major feature by the *New York Times*. He has also made appearances on Bloomberg TV and FOX news. In December 2014, Suspense Magazine named Zandri's, *THE SHROUD KEY*, as one of the "Best Books of 2014." Recently, *Suspense Magazine* selected *WHEN SHADOWS COME* as one of the "Best Books of 2016". A freelance photo-journalist and the author of the popular "lit blog," *The Vincent Zandri Vox*, Zandri has written for *Living Ready Magazine, RT, New York Newsday, Hudson Valley Magazine, The Times Union (Albany), Game & Fish Magazine,* and many more. He lives in Albany, New York. For more go to WWW.VINCENTZANDRI.COM

Vincent Zandri

Bear Media 2016

4 Orchard Grove, Albany, NY 12204

http://www.vincentzandri.com

Cover design by Elder Lemon Art

Author Photo by Jessica Painter

The characters and events portrayed in this book are fictitious. Any similarity to a real person, living or dead is coincidental and not intended by the author.

Published in the United States of America

Pieces of Mind

Made in United States
Troutdale, OR
02/04/2025

28664239R00202